WHAT THE ENEMY DOESN'T WANT YOU TO KNOW

THAT CAN CHANGE YOUR LIFE

MATT DALBEY

SEEK PRESS™

Sidestepped: What the Enemy Doesn't Want You to Know That Can Change Your Life
© 2022 Seek Press, LLC
Published by Seek Press, LLC
seekpress.us

All rights reserved. No part of this publication may be reproduced, distributed, or transmitted in any form or by any means, including photocopying, recording, or other electronic or mechanical methods, without the prior written permission of the publisher, except in the case of brief quotations embodied in critical reviews and certain other noncommercial uses permitted by copyright law.

First printing, 2022

Sidestepped™ is a trademark of Seek Press, LLC

ISBN: 979-8-9858365-0-9 (paperback)
ISBN: 979-8-9858365-1-6 (ebook)
ISBN: 979-8-9858365-2-3 (audiobook)

Unless otherwise indicated, scripture quotations are from the ESV® Bible (The Holy Bible, English Standard Version®), Copyright © 2001 by Crossway, a publishing ministry of Good News Publishers. Used by permission. All rights reserved.

Scripture taken from the New King James Version®. Copyright © 1982 by Thomas Nelson. Used by permission. All rights reserved.

Scripture quotations marked (NIV) are taken from the Holy Bible, New International Version®, NIV®. Copyright © 1973, 1978, 1984, 2011 by Biblica, Inc.® Used by permission of Zondervan. All rights reserved worldwide. www.zondervan.com The "NIV" and "New International Version" are trademarks registered in the United States Patent and Trademark Office by Biblica, Inc.®

Scripture quotations taken from the (NASB®) New American Standard Bible®, Copyright © 2020 by The Lockman Foundation. Used by permission. All rights reserved. www.lockman.org

Scripture quotations marked (NLT) are taken from the Holy Bible, New Living Translation, copyright ©1996, 2004, 2015 by Tyndale House Foundation. Used by permission of Tyndale House Publishers, Carol Stream, Illinois 60188. All rights reserved.

Scripture quotations marked (KJV) are from the King James Version of the Bible.

All emphasis in Scripture reference and other third-party quotations have been added by the author.

Book design by KUHN Design Group

Cover and interior design © 2022 Seek Press, LLC

DISCLAIMER

The publisher and the author are providing this book and its contents on an "as is" basis and make no representations or warranties of any kind with respect to this book or its contents. The publisher and the author disclaim all such representations and warranties. In addition, the publisher and the author assume no responsibility for errors, inaccuracies, omissions, or any other inconsistencies herein and hereby disclaim any liability to any party for any loss, damage, or disruption caused by errors or omissions, whether such errors or omissions result from negligence, accident, or any other cause. The events in the book are based on the author's memories and are from his perspective. All names have been changed or omitted to protect the identities of those involved.

This book is meant as a source of valuable information for the reader; it is not meant as a substitute for direct expert assistance. If such level of assistance is required, the services of a competent professional should be sought. The publisher and the author make no guarantees concerning the level of success you may experience by following the advice and strategies contained in this book, and you accept the risk that results will differ for each reader. The examples, advice, and strategies provided in this book may not be suitable for every situation or reader, and are not intended to represent or guarantee that you will achieve the same or similar results. The use of this book implies your acceptance of this disclaimer.

For my best friend Jesus, who never sidestepped the often misunderstood and uncomfortable realities of the opposing kingdoms of God and Satan (e.g., see Matt. 12:26-28).

For my wife, my other best friend and the most incredible woman on earth. Without her feedback and God-given gift of encouragement, this book would not exist.

For my children, who continue to mature in their love for Jesus and awareness of the unseen.

For anyone who has felt abandoned among the battles of life. You don't need to fight alone because God is "a very present help in trouble" (Ps. 46:1b ESV).

CONTENTS

Preface: *From worrying to warring* 9

Introduction: *How will you win your next battle?* 13

PART 1: CONQUERING FEAR
It's time to turn the tables on the enemy

1. Be Aware 21
2. Be Awake 41
3. Be Believing 51
4. Be Careful 65
5. Be Strong 77

PART 2: CRUSHING DISCOURAGEMENT
It's time to take courage from above

6. Discouragement Incapacitates 89
7. Encouragement Insulates and Ignites 101
8. Encouragement Breeds Encouragers 109

PART 3: COUNTERING THE ENEMY
It's time to defeat what defeats you

9. Come Burdened 121
10. Come Helpless 133
11. Come Indifferent 145
12. Come Distracted 155

Notes 179

Note to Reader: *Now what?* 181

PREFACE

FROM WORRYING TO WARRING

It was not my plan to author a book. But here it is.

It unexpectedly began one day when I was relaxing in a hot bath. What a therapeutic way to unwind after a long week. Not this time.

As I read in the Bible about those who exhibited extraordinary faith and courage, I felt something stirring in me. I then suddenly saw myself at the edge of a cliff. Jesus was standing behind me. Even though I didn't want to move from where I was, I could sense Him prodding me to "jump," to step off into a new and unknown season of life. (Although I didn't perceive it at the time, that season would include writing books.)

Well, I had a decision to make. I could say "yes" in submission to what Jesus was urging me to do. Or I could try to brush it aside. I immediately began thumbing through a myriad of what-if scenarios in my mind. Worry and fear filled my heart. Like many times before, God was asking me to trust in Him with all my heart rather than relying on my own limited understanding (see Prov. 3:5).

Thankfully, I said, "yes, I'm all in." Once I did, like Jeremiah, I felt "a burning fire" rising within me (see Jer. 20:9). Like the Israelites, the Lord my Shepherd was guiding me, speaking to me "from the midst of the fire" of His presence (see Deut. 4:12; John 10:27 NASB). And in that flame, my fear was being burned up "for our God is a consuming fire" (Heb. 12:29 NASB). The Spirit was heightening my awareness of the harsh reality of Satan's campaign to lay waste to lives everywhere. God was kindling courage to battle against an enemy I had been relatively oblivious to. The Father was stoking a zeal to help liberate spiritual captives. I was born again at a young age (and have grown in love with Jesus and people ever since). But that day in the bath, I got to "burn again" with a fresh and fiery passion to war for people, to resist the spiritual forces of evil, and to "Never be lacking in zeal, but keep your spiritual fervor, serving the Lord" (Rom. 12:11 NIV).

Like everything up to that point, what happened next completely surprised me. I got so fired up with righteous fury in opposition to the enemy that my hands literally curled up. Most of my facial muscles froze. My body became partially paralyzed. I initially wondered, "Am I having a stroke? Am I dying?" Barely able to speak, I mumbled to my wife to call

911. But although my mind and body couldn't reconcile what was happening, no matter how strange and unprecedented it felt, I sensed God's peace in my spirit. Thankfully, by the time the paramedics arrived, my condition had improved. There was no stroke. No medical issues. Everything checked out. That said, something did die that day. The best way I can try to convey what happened when I submitted to God's "next" for my life is by borrowing Jesus's metaphor from John 12:24, when He said, "Truly, truly, I say to you, unless a grain of wheat falls into the earth and dies, it remains alone; but if it dies, it bears much fruit."

Since that day, the Father's love has multiplied even more through me to those around me. And now, through this book, the fruit of what God awakened in me is being carried by His wind to others, including you. But just like fruit grows organically, not mechanically, what you're reading (or hearing) is a natural byproduct of countless interactions with Jesus. This book was not constructed so much as it was cultivated.

I could have never anticipated the full extent to which the forces of evil would resist me while writing a book about exposing and resisting their schemes. But the more the enemy pushed back, the more I wrote, and the more I shared God's love with others. My warrior King was literally training "my hands for war, and my fingers for battle" (Ps. 144:1b). Ironically, the "flaming darts of the evil one" only ignited me to fight back and to "in all circumstances take up the shield of faith" (see Eph. 6:16). Each opposition campaign of the devil presented me with an opportunity to joyfully offer myself "as a living sacrifice, holy and acceptable to God, which is your spiritual worship" (Rom. 12:1b). In the end, all of the enemy's attacks have backfired on him. Much of this book was born out of the spiritual battles I was born to fight... and win.

But even though you and I are designed to win battles and subdue spiritual foes, it does *not* mean that winning comes naturally. Even though battles abound and winning is possible, it does *not* mean that anyone actually wants to resist when it's time to fight.

INTRODUCTION

HOW WILL YOU WIN YOUR NEXT BATTLE?

Wham! My body slammed to the mat. Chest heaving, I struggled to catch my breath. In a moment, I was on my back. Before I realized what had happened, my rival had taken me down. He had defeated me with ease. Stunned, I slowly staggered to my feet.

I realized I had been inadvertently paired up with a wrestler from the wrong (i.e., heavier) weight class. This rookie wrestler was outmatched in every way. All of the other contenders in the room were bigger and stronger than me. To make things worse, I had little or no training before that wrestling match, if one could even call it that.

Although I was no older than seven or eight at the time, I will never forget the lessons my opponent quite literally pounded into me that day.

I learned that I would lose every time without the awareness and ability to win against my combatant. I am powerless and ill-equipped for victory without sufficient training beforehand. Without adequate preparation, defeat is inevitable.

In many ways, wrestling is like life. Even though life looks different for each of us, we *all* encounter various struggles and battles. But a spiritual dimension lies behind every human struggle (internal or external). There is a raging war in the shadows of our minds and hearts.

Ephesians 6:12 confirms that,

> "For we do *not* wrestle against flesh and blood, but against the rulers, against the authorities, against the *cosmic powers* over this present darkness, against *the spiritual forces of evil in the heavenly places*."

Even though the conflict referenced in Ephesians is common to us all, it is not for the faint-hearted. The Greek word translated "wrestle" can be defined as "a contest between two in which each endeavours to throw the other, and which is decided when the victor is able to hold his opponent down with his hand upon his neck."[1]

Any professional athlete or soldier is acutely aware of the necessity of acquiring the proper training well before engaging their opponent. And any time you are unprepared, I am unprepared, to wrestle our common enemy, we will get taken to the mat. God directed the human authors of Scripture to employ various synonyms when enlightening us about the enemy. Some of which include the devil, your adversary, Satan, the tempter, the evil one, the angel of light, spiritual forces of evil, demons, demonic spirits, etc. (see 1 Pet. 5:8-9; 2 Cor. 2:11; Matt. 4:3; Matt. 6:13 NKJV; 2 Cor. 11:14; Eph. 6:12; Matt. 4:24; Rev. 16:14). Likewise, I also use the same singular and plural terminologies interchangeably throughout this book. But regardless of how we refer to him, to them, to win against the enemy *during* battle, we *must* first put on the whole armor of God *before* we are pounded by the *next* demonic onslaught (see Eph. 6:11, 13). That's right, resisting Satan is *not* a one-and-done event. We are in a lifelong battle.

Because the process of "being sanctified" is ongoing (see Heb. 10:14), so also is the directive to "resist the devil" (see James 4:7 NIV). The two are interdependent. When our advancement against the enemy stalls, so does our sanctification. As such, the discipline of how to fight and win spiritual battles deserves our utmost attention. Yet ironically, two of the most commonly sidestepped *biblical* subjects I've observed spanning four decades are: the believer's *one* enemy and the *one* thing we all need more than anything to stand firm against him (see Eph. 6:12, 10). I explore both sides of that coin in this book, which culminates in chapter 12—so you'll want to read through to the end.

No one is born or even born again, intuitively knowing how to withstand the evil one. Nor is anyone particularly thrilled to leap back to their proverbial feet, especially after getting knocked down by the enemy. It isn't easy, and it doesn't come naturally. It is a learned skill that this book will help you develop, regardless of where you are in your Christian walk.

As you read or listen to what I've written, I pray that you will be gifted something more valuable than knowledge alone. More than a data transfer from one person to another, my goal is to instill courage in you to fight and win the war hiding all around us. And more than collecting more knowledge, Paul's prayer for the Ephesians is also my prayer for you: that you would "know the love of Christ *that surpasses knowledge*" (see Eph. 3:19). The reality is that the courage to resist demonic forces flows from abiding in Jesus's love. More about that later on.

I sincerely hope that these words prove to be timely spoken (see Prov. 15:23) and that they help you lay hold of the courage you were born to walk in. May God use this book to "en-courage" you at just the right time as you face whatever you are up against. I am rooting for you! Jesus is rooting for you!

This is the first and foundational book in a series; it sets the stage for subsequent releases. Each forthcoming work will help you identify and overcome covert strategies of the enemy—strategies aimed at ruining your life and neutralizing your effectiveness for God.

How will you win your next battle?

Each day, you and I are either moving forward or falling back. Practically speaking, we are either winning or losing. Whenever we opt *not* to push back, we will be pushed back.

There is no spiritual demilitarized zone—at least not in this life. If a foreign invader attacked and infiltrated your country, would pretending that there was no war make the war go away? Of course not. So also, simply because you wish the devil would leave you alone without a fight on your part doesn't mean that he will. Like a massive breaking ocean wave, diving in headfirst is always better than trying to outrun it. Turning tail just gets you pummeled and prolongs the pain. Wishing won't repel the devil but opposing him will. "Resist the devil, and he *will* flee from you" (James 4:7b NIV)… this is God's promise to us, *but it is conditional.* It is an if-then statement. If, *and only if*, you choose to resist the devil, will he flee from you. But if it's that simple, why aren't more people pushing back against the kingdom of darkness? Because the topic is so often avoided, many individuals don't see the need to resist the devil or don't want to. Others are unaware that they're in the spiritual battle of their lives. As a result, many haven't been adequately trained on how to fight.

But endeavoring to win your battles begins with seeing what is unseen. It's time to discern what's going on behind the scenes, what's hiding beyond our visible world. Our daily victories will always stem from our awareness of that greater reality (see 2 Cor. 4:18).

PART 1

CONQUERING FEAR

*It's time to turn the
tables on the enemy*

CHAPTER 1

BE AWARE

"Then Elisha prayed and said, 'O LORD, please open his eyes that he may see.' So the LORD opened the eyes of the young man, and he saw, and behold, the mountain was full of horses and chariots of fire all around Elisha."

2 KINGS 6:17

The mind of the king of Syria was greatly troubled" (2 Kings 6:11a) because Israel was continually foiling even his most covert military strikes. He was furious. Someone must have leaked confidential intel to the enemy, or so the King presumed. He suspected a mole in his administration. Then an unexpected revelation surfaced.

> "And the mind of the king of Syria was greatly troubled because of this thing, and he called his servants and said to them, 'Will you not show me who of us is for the king of Israel?' And one of his servants said, 'None, my lord, O king; but Elisha, the prophet who is in Israel, tells the King

of Israel the words that you speak in your bedroom.' And he said, 'Go and see where he is, that I may send and seize him.' It was told him, 'Behold, he is in Dothan.' So he sent there horses and chariots and a great army, and they came by night and surrounded the city" (2 Kings 6:11-13).

Although not present, Elisha heard—through the Spirit of God—every private plot of the eighth century BC Syrian King, Ben-Hadad[2] (as identified by name in 2 Kings 6:24).

SIGHT TO FIGHT

Once Ben-Hadad realized why he kept losing battles, Elisha became the target of the King's retaliation. He sent his army to seize Elisha. It wasn't long before hostile enemy forces surrounded the city. As he looked upon the Syrian army all around, Elisha's servant (Gehazi) became overcome with fear. He was keenly aware of their intense anger, their numbers, their strength. Paralyzed by fear, Gehazi was at a loss for what to do.

But, as the story continues in 2 Kings 6:16-18, Elisha's awareness of a greater reality prompted a powerful counter-offensive.

> "He said, 'Do not be afraid, for those who are with us are more than those who are with them.' Then Elisha prayed and said, 'O LORD, please open his eyes that he may see.' So the LORD opened the eyes of the young man, and he saw, and behold, the mountain was full of horses and chariots of fire all around Elisha. And when the Syrians came

down against him, Elisha prayed to the LORD and said, 'Please strike this people with blindness.' So he struck them with blindness in accordance with the prayer of Elisha."

With an awareness of the unseen, Elisha saw the God of Armies who surrounded the Syrian army. The visible warriors of earth were no match for the invisible armies of Heaven. Elisha opened his mouth to summon the Lord's help in full realization of this. At that moment, something happened. A tangible life-altering victory was won. Despite being incredibly outnumbered, a lone unarmed civilian neutralized the might of an invading military. Astounding.

But even more impressive than a single victory was what sustained that victory long-term. Elisha led his assailants back to the King of Israel while they were still blind, where they became surrounded. The tables had been turned. But instead of killing those who hated him, Elisha showed them mercy and grace. Instead of cursing them, he prayed for their eyes to be opened and blessed them with a lavish feast (see 2 Kings 6:20-23)! To quote directly from 2 Kings 6:23,

> "So he prepared for them a great feast, and when they had eaten and drunk, he sent them away, and they went to their master. And the Syrians did not come again on raids into the land of Israel."

Elisha did not launch any physical arrows nor throw a single spear. Instead, the single ultimate Power in the universe responded to a single prayer to overpower the enemy. The demonic powers that previously held sway over Elisha's haters were initially broken through prayer and then kept at bay through the power of love. The high King of Heaven intervened when the visible, natural universe offered no defense for Elisha. God neutralized Elisha's foes without them seeing what had hit them, all by an unexpected one-two blow of temporary blindness followed by transformative kindness. Interestingly, several hundred years later, God used a similar approach to win over Saul of Tarsus (see Acts 9). The Lord sometimes goes to great and gracious lengths to peel back what is visible to reveal what would otherwise remain invisible.

With all he had seen as a servant of a great man of God, it's ironic that Gehazi was oblivious to what Elisha so clearly saw all around in the Spirit. Like Elisha's servant, many today are blind to behold the unseen reality always in play everywhere.

I get it. If we can't see something, it is easy to forget or deny its existence. Out of sight, out of mind. But, like for Elisha and Gehazi, the opposing forces of good and evil are still constantly clashing all around us. And to fight right, we first need the right sight.

CONSCIOUS TO FIGHT

Irrespective of one's religious beliefs, documented and undocumented encounters with the spirit realm are ubiquitous throughout human history. For example, Jesus's most outspoken theological opponents (the Pharisees) acknowledged the existence of angels, the spiritual part of a person, and even the linkage between demons and mental disorders (see Acts 23:8; John 10:20-21).

Well-aware of society's growing fascination with spiritual things, namely anything demonic, the film industry certainly hasn't shied away from producing record numbers of horror films.[3] As the number three ranked movie genre, horror grossed over half a billion dollars in the year before this book was first published,[4] equating to a 135% increase year-over-year.[5] And that's not even counting the spiritual undertones woven into the non-horror TV and movie genres. According to Pew Research, "Americans are turning to television instead of God since the pandemic started, *with Christians being the top religious affiliation to do so.*"[6]

I have observed a striking phenomenon among some Christian circles: the topic of the devil and demons has become mostly taboo. Hundreds of millions attend traditional evangelical Christian churches worldwide,[7] and that phenomenon is observable in many of them. Yet ironically, what is enjoyed in the living room Monday through Saturday has become off-limits in the sanctuary on Sunday.

In the void left by many Christian preachers and influencers, Hollywood educates believers and nonbelievers alike with a skewed view of spiritual realities.

Despite the ever-present existence of the spirit world, many believers behave as if it is fanciful or, at a minimum, not very relevant to them. I have met many in the Church who are uncomfortable, even fearful, discussing anything of a demonic nature. Try talking about the devil, demons, or the spirit realm, and many will scramble to change the subject. They largely avoid such discussions because they claim they don't want to give Satan too much attention. But I wonder if what's really going on is the demons hanging around such individuals are horrified of being exposed and expelled from their human hiding places.

I agree that we shouldn't be *overly* devil conscious. But neither should we be "devil *un*conscious." The biblical imperative is that we "*Stay alert! Watch out* for your great enemy, the devil. He prowls around like a roaring lion, looking for someone to devour" (1 Peter 5:8 NLT). If Scripture is clear that we should be alert and watchful about the enemy, how then have so many become convinced of a contradictory counternarrative? Although perhaps well-meaning, much of the Church has pushed the spiritual awareness pendulum to the opposite extreme and into unbiblical territory. To avoid demonic obsession, many have veered off the cliff of demonic obliviousness. Putting their heads in the sand has left many believers ignorant of Satan's schemes, in direct contradiction to 2 Corinthians 2:11 (NASB)—"So that no advantage would be taken of us by Satan, for we are *not ignorant* of his schemes."

Meanwhile, the devil is taking every occasion to use our ignorance against us. If we are unaware that Satan is the one striking us, we will be more prone to "beat up" ourselves or others in response.... *instead* of wrestling the real enemy (as God says we should do in Ephesians 6:12). Make no mistake, we all fight. But tragically, we often end up fighting anyone but the true enemy. And that enemy has no qualms about disguising himself as God, a family member, a friend, a stranger, or even you. If you're confused about who's really attacking you, you won't know who to fight. The evil one would rather you turn on anyone but him. Instead of being unified against him, the devil has pitted people against God, others, and often themselves.

For example, although it may sometimes *seem* as if you're wrestling your "old self," that is impossible because "we know that *our old self was crucified* with him in order that the body of sin might be brought to *nothing*" (Rom. 6:6a). Paul conveyed the same message to the Galatian believers: "I have been crucified with Christ. It is no longer I who live, but Christ who lives in me" (Gal. 2:20a). Your old nature has been replaced with Jesus's nature because Jesus now lives in you. You have a new identity. To the Colossians (3:3), Paul reiterated that "For you *have died*, and your life is hidden with Christ in God" (notice that "have died" is past tense). No wonder he also wrote to the Ephesians that "we do *not* wrestle against flesh and blood" but instead "against the spiritual forces of evil in the heavenly places" (see Eph. 6:12). Even though Satan plays off our physical bodily desires, our old spiritual self is dead. When Christ was crucified, "he died to sin, *once for all*," so also all true believers died once—"one has died for all, therefore all have died" (see Rom. 6:10; 2 Cor. 5:14).

Based on the existence of your new self *presently*, because "you have been raised with Christ," is how you and I are even able to "seek the things that are above" (see Col. 3:1) and "live self-controlled, upright, and godly lives in the present age" (Titus 2:12b). Even if it *feels* like we are fighting our flesh at times, the Bible brings us back to what's true: "You, however, *are not in the flesh* but in the Spirit, if in fact the Spirit of God dwells in you. Anyone who does not have the Spirit of Christ does not belong to him" (Rom. 8:9). Does God's Spirit dwell in you? If so, then you *aren't* fighting you.

According to Scripture, there is *no* such thing as the coexistence of the old *and* the new—only old *or* new. *No* yin and yang. Despite what is parroted among many Christian leaders, you *don't* have a white dog *and* a black dog cohabiting you. "For you *were once* darkness," (past tense) "*but now you are light in the Lord*" (present tense)—and, as a result, we now have the power to "live as children of light" (future tense) (Eph. 5:8 NIV). The only black dog left to wrestle is the devil; he is our "adversary" (singular) (see 1 Pet. 5:8; Eph. 6:12). The day the White Dog (i.e., Holy Spirit) came to reside in you, you became the "clean and white" bride of Christ—"And to her was granted that she should be arrayed in fine linen, *clean and white*: for the fine linen is the righteousness of saints" (Rev. 19:8 KJV).

So complete was the work of the Cross that Jesus didn't just pretty us up; He made us new. Jesus doesn't rehab us. He instead demoed our old self and is building something completely new from the ground up (see 1 Pet. 2:5). Even though what God is forming in the new you is not yet complete, the old you is *completely* six feet under. While God's "good work in you" will remain a work in process until "the day of Jesus Christ" (see Phil. 1:6), there is *no* need for you to recrucify what's already dead… Jesus already did that for you. This is gospel 101. Little surprise that the deceiver has cast confusion on it. Today, if you are "a new creation" in Christ (see 2 Cor. 5:17 NKJV), don't let Satan convince you otherwise.

Ironically, the one group (Christians) who possesses the ultimate Truth source (the Bible) about our only real enemy (the devil) often sidesteps and muddies realities as clearly laid out in Scripture as anything else. Has any part of Scripture changed or expired since written? No, not according to Peter (see 1 Pet. 1:25), who quoted Isaiah (40:8): "The grass withers, the flower fades, but the word of our God will stand *forever*." Jesus even issued a warning to anyone who downplays or dismisses (i.e., "relaxes") *any* of God's words (see Matt. 5:18-19).

Did the unseen spirit world cease to exist when Jesus ascended to Heaven? The Gospels, Acts, and other New Testament writings affirm otherwise. Is the demonic activity in the world declining, or is it on the rise? Has Satan stopped harassing people? You decide.

In all actuality, what has become taboo among much of the Church is perhaps more timely than ever. If God, in His timeless Word, does not consider the topic of demons strange or unmentionable, then neither should we... especially if we believe in Jesus.

Do you believe in Jesus? Jesus plainly prophesied, "And these signs *will* accompany *those who believe*: in my name *they will cast out demons*; they will speak in new tongues" (Mark 16:17). Since Jesus cast out demons, among other things (e.g., see Mark 1:21-39), so should we. To again quote Jesus, "Truly, truly, I say to you, *whoever believes in me will also do the works that I do*; and greater works than these will he do, because I am going to the Father" (John 14:12).

Regardless of where your beliefs are on the theological spectrum, you carry Satan's kryptonite. If you believe in Jesus, you carry something—more accurately, Someone—far more powerful than Satan. As a born-again believer, you get to say, "I have been crucified with Christ. It is no longer I who live, but *Christ who lives in me*" (Gal. 2:20a). And because Jesus now lives in believers through the Holy Spirit, we have "become partakers of the divine nature" (see 2 Pet. 1:4).

CLUED-IN TO FIGHT

So are you immune from demonic harassment as long as Jesus lives in you? Did Satan and his minions decide to leave you alone the moment you were born again? Many of the Christians I have known throughout four decades as a follower of Christ talk and often live as if the answer is yes.

Much of the Church believes that the devil will *only* bother you if you are either unsaved or steeped in some outwardly grotesque sin. If we are walking closely with Jesus, loving Him, serving others, seemingly doing well, then the demonic forces of evil will leave us alone—right?

Theoretically speaking, what if we were morally perfect? If that were true, would the forces of evil still target us? Yes, absolutely. Matthew 4:1 says, "Then Jesus," who is perfect, "was led up by the Spirit into the wilderness." Why was He led into the wilderness? "To be tempted by the devil." Jesus was perfect, yet Beelzebub still bombarded him—he "departed from" Jesus, only to return at "an opportune time" (see Luke 4:13b).

If Jesus, the Perfect One, was not immune from spiritual attack, then neither am I, neither are you, and neither is anyone. Since Satan came against Jesus, we shouldn't be surprised when he comes against any of Jesus's followers. Case in point, Jesus said, "Simon, Simon, Satan has asked to sift *all of you* as wheat" (Luke 22:31 NIV). On another occasion, Jesus directly confronted the devil, who was working in the mind and mouth of one of His disciples: "Jesus turned and said to Peter, 'Get behind me, Satan! You are a stumbling block to me; you do not have in mind the concerns of God, but merely human concerns'" (Matt. 16:23 NIV).

Instead of acknowledging and dealing with the demonic head-on as Jesus did, many believe the false narrative that it is better to ignore it. I used to be of this persuasion, *but without even realizing it*. I wasn't yet clued-in to the subtleties of how anti-biblical that mindset is.

Sadly, this way of thinking and living is as prevalent in the Church as it is subtle. I call this mindset the *Fallacy of Demonic Immunity*. I believe that such a perspective is often ultimately rooted in fear and pride. Fear of the demonic and fear-based pride about what others might think if they knew that demons were oppressing them. We must shun such fear-based reasoning because the "fear of man will prove to be a snare" (Prov. 29:25a NIV). But instead of finding greater freedom, the enemy uses fear to ensnare and encage anyone who falls under its influence.

To those who, knowingly or unknowingly, have been in the *Fallacy of Demonic Immunity* camp, I would pose the question: for whom then is the spiritual armor of Ephesians 6? To whom was the letter of Ephesians written? Paul addressed it to born-again believers. If there is no battle, then why do we need armor? If being saved renders us insusceptible to satanic salvos, then why does Paul tell us to put on the very "armor *of God*" (see Eph. 6:11)!?

Since God warns His Church *as a whole* to "give no opportunity to the devil" (see in Eph. 4:27), *no one*—regardless of their role or position—is excluded from demonic influence. If being Jesus's disciples exempts us from being embattled by the evil one, then why did Jesus teach His disciples to pray "deliver us from the evil one" daily (see Matt. 6:13 NKJV)? Because that's what we need.

We are *not* safe from demonic attacks simply because we belong to Jesus. Not at all. I want to voice that loud and clear. Satan is called the accuser of whom? "Our brothers and sisters," the Church (see Rev. 12:10 NIV). Becoming born again does not exclude anyone from temptation, sin, or Satan. When you joined God's family, you also joined His army. Paul definitively stated in Ephesians 6:12 that *we* are the ones who wrestle against the demonic. Our heavenly commander-in-chief is not the only one who fights; He has also enlisted us as His soldiers.

While God is always ready to fight for us and with us, Satan will never stop fighting us. As long as we are in the devil's temporary domain (earth in its current state), he will never tire of targeting us. He doesn't even care that we may not be prepared to resist him. Our enemy most prefers to strike when we are least prepared. Rain or shine, day or night, ready or not, like it or not, our adversary is relentless in his assaults. He shows mercy to no one.

The reality is that *everyone*, Christian or not, is harassed and influenced by the devil more often than we fully realize. Yet the deceiver has deceived many believers into believing that demons only bother unbelievers. This is an ingenious and sinister scheme on Satan's part because it allows him to run amok unchecked. He strategically camouflages himself because he is painfully aware of your God-given power and authority over him (even if you aren't).

Would you want your enemies (us) to know what you were up to if you were the devil? Of course not. He wants us to stay fuzzy, or better yet, oblivious about his plans. Who do you suppose is ultimately behind catchy one-liners cautioning us not to be too "devil aware"? Specifically, as it pertains to our unseen enemy, God has given all born-again believers clear imperatives to be alert and watchful, resist and wrestle, pray for deliverance, and cast out demons. The dark one who "disguises himself as an angel of light" (see 2 Cor. 11:14) is allowed to hide among many Christians' lives because those same individuals deny that he is meddling in the mix. Would you fight (or resist) an enemy you *didn't* perceive as a real threat to you? Probably not. Neither would I.

Do you possibly have opinions and mindsets contrary to "the knowledge of God" (see 2 Cor. 10:5)? Who doesn't, right?! Consistent with the language of his classic spiritual warfare passage (see Eph. 6:10-20), in 2 Corinthians 10:3-5, Paul referred to such mindsets as demonic strongholds.

> "For though we walk in the flesh, we are not waging war according to the flesh. For the weapons of our warfare are not of the flesh but have divine power to destroy strongholds. We destroy arguments and every lofty opinion raised against the knowledge of God, and take every thought captive to obey Christ."

Strongholds are the mindsets and thought patterns behind which we (knowingly or unknowingly) harbor the demonic. They are the areas of unnecessary spiritual bondage and mental baggage in our lives. The challenge is recognizing where they are hiding and then getting rid of them once they've been identified.

Note that Paul did *not* call those lofty mindsets "weakholds." Taking a wrecking ball to long-standing strongholds will never be easy or painless. In fact, the longer any stronghold has remained fused to your psyche, the more effort (i.e., persistence, time, energy) it might take to dismantle. Nevertheless, doing so is both necessary and attainable. We "have *divine power* to *destroy* strongholds" (see 2 Cor. 10:4)! And even before the dust settles, you will be amazed at what God is ready to help you build in their place.

Replete with Scripture references, think of this book as heavy machinery to help you obliterate strongholds for yourself and others.

READY TO FIGHT

I was immersed in fervent prayer late one night. In the words of Paul, I was keeping "alert with all perseverance, making supplication for all the saints" (Eph. 6:18b). With God very present in the room, I sensed the Father's love-driven fury compelling me to intercede for one of His (adult) children. Well aware that Jesus has given us "power and authority over *all demons*" (see Luke 9:1), I bound and cast out the demons I perceived were harassing a fellow believer. Even though the person I was interceding for was unaware of my late-night warring, the God who never sleeps heard my petitions and fought with me.

No one taught me to do what I just described, to deal with demonic forces remotely. No one on earth anyway. I certainly didn't read any instructional books on the topic. No, the best Teacher of all, the Holy Spirit, unexpectedly put it in my heart in mid-prayer. It was His idea, not mine. It only occurred to me afterward that Jesus also did the same sort of thing from afar (for example, see Mark 7:29-30). I simply acted on what God impressed upon my heart at the moment… and it worked (as it has many other times).

Starting the next day, I witnessed something I had rarely seen in that particular Christian. Newfound freedom and joy.

Just one day after that, I encountered something strange. Or, more accurately, something strange encountered me. A completely different individual began acting uncharacteristically aggressive and manic towards me for no *apparent* reason. It seems as if I had stirred up an unseen hornet's nest. I became the target of demonic retaliation due to the freedom won for another Christian the day before. Don't assume you're doing something wrong because you're in the devil's crosshairs. It might be the exact opposite. Satan will often assault you when you're doing something right—when he perceives you are or could become a more significant threat to him. Any time you help free spiritual captives or experience greater

Be Aware

freedom yourself, expect the enemy to pitch a fit and fight back. He's a sore loser. Have you ever felt agitated or angry towards someone but didn't know why? If so, you were probably unknowingly influenced by an evil spirit who wanted to "get at" someone else through you.

Well, can you guess what I did later that evening? I battled privately on behalf of the second individual, just like I had for the other person two days earlier. I prayed with authority while acting on Jesus's words that "whatever you bind on earth will be bound in heaven" (see Matt. 16:19 NIV). In the same way Jesus commanded Satan to "be gone" and regularly rebuked evil spirits (e.g., see Matt. 4:10; Mark 1:25; 9:25), I also told the demons to leave that second Christian alone.

That same person was very kind and calm by the following day, in stark contrast to the previous 24-hour period. A spiritual battle had been won literally overnight.

On another occasion, I met with a man who loves Jesus. Demons were tormenting him. But the same day I helped him break free from his demonic oppressors, my preschool-aged son became the target of the enemy. Suddenly, my boy began to complain of pain throughout his body. At one point, he even told me that he felt something invisible choking him. I should mention that my son has never experienced anything like that before or since.

I quickly sprang into action to fight for my little guy. But after praying for him with little or no improvement, the Holy Spirit directed me to have my son cry out to Jesus. The moment he simply said, "Jesus help!" I immediately perceived Jesus's powerful presence in the room. I was so instantly enveloped in God's unmistakable joy that I involuntarily started laughing with glee. A few minutes later, all of my son's pain had completely vanished. It is notable that even before seeing any improvement in my little boy, Jesus first came and flooded my heart with the sheer joy of Him. Read Jesus's dialogue with some of His disciples in Luke 10:17-20.

> "The seventy-two returned with joy, saying, 'Lord, even the demons are subject to us in your name!' And he said to them, 'I saw Satan fall like lightning from heaven. Behold, I have given you authority to tread on serpents and scorpions, and over all the power of the enemy, and nothing shall hurt you. *Nevertheless, do not rejoice in this, that the spirits are subject to you, but rejoice that your names are written in heaven.*'"

Rejoicing "that your names are written in heaven" is synonymous with remembering to put on the "helmet of salvation" (from *The Whole Armor of God* Ephesians 6 passage). Even though it is our imperative to resist the devil, our ultimate joy is not derived from the war itself but from the eternal life won for us by the "man of war; the LORD is His name" (Exod. 15:3 NKJV).

I have had many other encounters like those I just shared in which the armies of the Almighty rushed in to fight for me, my family, my friends, and even strangers. And in each instance, I have been compelled to worship the Father for His goodness, help, strength, and salvation. Every time, victory was just a prayer away, a word away, an act of love away. But to fight in the first place, I needed to be awakened to what's at stake at the hands of our ruthless rival, the devil.

CHAPTER 2

BE AWAKE

"Be sober-minded; be watchful. Your adversary the devil prowls around like a roaring lion, seeking someone to devour."

1 PETER 5:8

Regardless of what we *want* to do in response to what's transpiring in the invisible world, what does God say we *should* do? Should we ignore it? Not according to Peter. He charged the Church to "Be sober-minded; be watchful. Your adversary the devil prowls around like a roaring lion, seeking someone to devour" (1 Pet. 5:8).

A MATTER OF URGENCY

Like Elisha, we still encounter conflicts in the twenty-first century. Our world is being torn apart in many ways by an unseen world. Our unseen enemy is devoted to devastating as many human lives as possible. Can you see it? Regardless of his various tactics, the enemy's endgame is to drag as many people to Hell as possible. Jesus revealed that "*the devil comes and takes away the word from their hearts, so that they may not believe and be saved*" (Luke 8:12b NIV). And one way Satan prevents souls from being saved is by neutralizing those going to Heaven from rescuing those headed for Hell.

As "the deceiver of the *whole* world" (see Rev. 12:9), Satan's insidious influence is everywhere. His lies even permeate places where we would least expect them—more on that topic in the sequel to this book.

When we ignore the reality of our common enemy's influence as "the prince of the power of the air" (see Eph. 2:2), we neglect our responsibility to continue Jesus's mission to "set at liberty those who are oppressed" (see Luke 4:18). When we look the other way, away from this spiritual absolute, we turn from people who are harassed and imprisoned, who God wants to set free *through us*.

The purpose of spiritual warfare is to break out spiritual captives. Effective spiritual warfare isn't a fight against people; it's a fight for them. God's intent is for spiritual warfare to be a team sport. We get to advance together as a military unit, shoulder-to-shoulder with other believers who are also aware of what's at stake. Of course, you may experience seasons of life when it feels like you are the lone soldier taking a hill because, sadly, the soldiers around you are often out cold. It is my prayer that the Holy Spirit uses this book to expose some of what Satan has concealed from so many sleeping soldiers.

> "Therefore it says, 'Awake, O sleeper, and arise from the dead, and Christ will shine on you.' Look carefully then how you walk, not as unwise but as wise, making the best use of the time, because the days are evil" (Eph. 5:14b-16).

"The days are evil." No wonder so many individuals are riddled with anxiety, fear, and internal struggles. But we don't have to stay where we've been. We have a calling to be aware, awake, and alert. It's time to be compelled with the same love that moved Jesus to action.

A MATTER OF LIFE AND DEATH

You and I are in an invisible struggle with very visible, real, and lasting ramifications. There is a popular notion that invisible equates to inconsequential. It's time to trash that myth like the garbage it is. What did Jesus say about the unseen part of a person?

> "The good person out of the good treasure of his heart produces good, and the evil person out of his evil treasure produces evil, for *out of the abundance of the heart his mouth speaks*" (Luke 6:45).

What is invisible sooner or later becomes visible in a person's words and actions. James posed the following question (in James 4:1 NIV):

> "What causes fights and quarrels among you? Don't they come from your desires that *battle within you*?"

In the subsequent verses (2-3), he essentially explained that all self-serving external wars are first festering internal wars. Even though concealed below the surface, internal conflicts have external consequences. One real-life manifestation of how this plays out every day is in the form of suicide. There are more than 120 suicides *every day* in the U.S. alone.[8] How many people commit suicide due to inward and invisible thoughts and feelings? One hundred percent. Experts have called mortality from suicide, drug overdoses, and alcoholism "deaths of despair."[9] Despair is inward and invisible. Suicide is outward and visible. (Sometimes, it's good to state the obvious).

All life and death hang in the balance based on what is invisible. Yet our default temptation is to underestimate or doubt the power of what we can't see. But the more we win the hidden internal battles, the more we will find success in our external battles. Everything we don't see actually impacts everything we do see. This is not a new reality. Hebrews 11:3 says, "By faith we understand that the universe was created by the word of God, so that what is seen was not made out of things that are visible." Did you catch that? What we see with our eyes was not made from visible things. The invisible is the seed of everything visible.

Not only was the universe created by an unseen God, but new spiritual life in Christ is born from an unseen God. Jesus explained this reality to the high-ranking leader Nicodemus in John 3:5. "Jesus answered, 'Truly, truly, I say to you, unless one is born of water and the Spirit,'"—the Spirit of God is unseen—"'he cannot enter the kingdom of God.'"

The genesis of all visible and invisible-made-visible life in the universe is unseen. The Kingdom of God is unseen, but its effects always become seen. Proof of its existence is evidenced by its impact on the visible universe. This is precisely what Jesus went on to explain to Nicodemus.

> "That which is born of the flesh is flesh, and that which is born of the Spirit is spirit. Do not marvel that I said to you, 'You must be born again.' The wind blows where it wishes, and you hear its sound, but you do not know where it comes from or where it goes. So it is with everyone who is born of the Spirit" (John 3:6-8).

Any of us who have been born of the Spirit have been born of something unseen. God breathed, and you became. Everything physical originates from the metaphysical. You can't see the wind, but it alters what it encounters. What Elisha confronted in the eighth century BC was no exception. Even while new life springs from the unseen, the destruction of life is also rooted in that same invisible realm.

A MATTER FOR US ALL

At this point, maybe you are thinking, "Well, of course, Satan is real. I know that I have an unseen enemy. So what?"

I would ask the question: what are you doing to counter the devil's work (which is rampant everywhere)?

Maybe you don't think it's "your place." "Leave that stuff to ministry professionals," others may have led you to believe. Or the line of thinking might be something like, "Well, that was just for Jesus, but not for me. If Jesus has already won the victory, then I don't need to do anything. Do I?"

True, Jesus already did what only He could do; by providing the only way by which anyone can have eternal life. At the same time, He has also given us quite a bit to do. According to Acts 1:1b (and many other Bible passages), God has commissioned His people to continue "all that Jesus *began* to do and teach." Notice the word "began." Jesus started something. We get to carry on what He initiated as "imitators of God, as beloved children" (see Eph. 5:1). If there is nothing for us to do, then Paul would not have written the following in Romans 10:14 (NLT):

> "But how can they call on him to save them unless they believe in him? And how can they believe in him if they have never heard about him? *And how can they hear about him unless someone tells them?*"

You have been born into a battle. God is summoning you to engage in something very real. It's not a matter of if you *want* to be in this unseen battle. It's an unconventional battle, but a real battle nonetheless. You are already square in the middle of it, even as you read this book.

I have a choice. You have a choice. Like Gehazi, will we let the darkness we see overwhelm and paralyze us? Or will we shift our gaze to Jesus and find ourselves overwhelmed by Him, fearless to fight in the presence of the Light of the World!?

In the day-to-day, will we resist and prevail against the devil in light of what Jesus did to liberate us? Or will we live as if we are still captives of the demonic fear so prevalent throughout our planet?

> "Since therefore the children share in flesh and blood, he himself likewise partook of the same things, that through death he might destroy the one who has the power of death, that is, the devil, and deliver *all* those who through fear of death were subject to lifelong slavery" (Heb. 2:14-15).

Will we hang onto the Satanic fear that only takes from us? Or will we receive what our heavenly Father has already given us?

> "For you did *not* receive the spirit of slavery to fall back into fear, but you have received the Spirit of adoption as sons, by whom we cry, 'Abba! Father!'" (Rom. 8:15)

> "For God has *not* given us a spirit of fear, but of power and of love and of a sound mind" (2 Tim. 1:7 NKJV).

So, how are you going to fight? I say you might as well fight well because… it's truly a matter of life and death! We cannot ignore the unseen spiritual conflict raging around us without real and lasting consequences. Your life, my life, is not a dress rehearsal. You are living the real deal right now. Today there is a real battle for real souls, real people whom God deeply loves. For you, your family members, friends, coworkers, strangers on the street… for everyone.

We see people differently when we "See what great love the Father has lavished on us, that we should be called children of God" (1 John 3:1a NIV).

When we remember that "He who did not spare his own Son, but gave him up for us all" (Rom. 8:32a NIV), we find that "Christ's love compels us" (see 2 Cor. 5:14 NIV) also to give ourselves in love to others.

When we forget how to love, we can learn again because "This is how we know what love is: Jesus Christ laid down his life for us. And we ought to lay down our lives for our brothers and sisters" (1 John 3:16 NIV).

When we cannot muster up love, we must remind ourselves that love never came from us in the first place. Instead, "We love because [God] first loved us" (1 John 4:19 NIV).[10]

When fear fills our hearts at the thought of continuing what Jesus started (see Acts 1:1b) because we feel incapable, that's because we are. On our own anyway. Thankfully, "If you then, though you are evil, know how to give good gifts to your children, how much more will your Father in heaven give the Holy Spirit to those who ask him!" (Luke 11:13 NIV). Like Jesus's early disciples, we need the Holy Spirit's help (see Acts 1:4-5).

CHAPTER 3

BE BELIEVING

"But Caleb quieted the people before Moses and said, 'Let us go up at once and occupy it, for we are well able to overcome it.'"

NUMBERS 13:30

Our backyard "rough it" camping excursion was over. It was time to disassemble the tent and take the long trek home… across the yard. An air mattress and easy access to every modern convenience. We had suffered much staying in such a rugged place.

One of my daughters helped me pack up the tent on that particular occasion. I enjoy working on projects with my kids, but things were slow going this time on my daughter's part. Things would have undoubtedly gone much quicker, except for one thing. She was very distracted. She was distracted by all the scary bugs she saw creeping and scurrying among the blades of grass beneath her feet. For every insect she saw, the more she looked for them. The more she had an eye to see all the creepy-crawlies, the more they *seemed* to brush her feet and magically fly up into her hair. The more she meditated on how scary the bugs were, the more her mind made mountains out of molehills.

I explained all the logical reasons why there was nothing to fear. But it was too late. My daughter was already convinced she could do nothing about all those frightening creatures. She tiptoed and darted around as if with an invisible dancer, trying to avoid (what seemed to me) even the grass itself. Squealing and shrieking with nearly every step. Because she was paralyzed by what she perceived all around her, she became ineffective for "assignment tent break down." Any instructions about helping break down the tent were lost to the wind.

To me, it seemed silly that she was afraid of such harmless pests, pests that she could squash underfoot. But to her, the fear she *felt* was real. It didn't occur to her at that moment that there was an effective way to neutralize the threat. That backyard camping experience reminded me of a well-known Bible story.

DEFEATED BY POOR PERSPECTIVE

You might be familiar with the story of The Twelve Spies from Numbers 13 and 14. God had directed Moses to send

12 leaders of Israel—one from each tribe—to spy on the land of Canaan. God promised to give land to the Israelite people, but they didn't yet possess what He had promised. After viewing the land, here is the majority report from ten of the spies:

> "At the end of forty days they returned from spying out the land. And they came to Moses and Aaron and to all the congregation of the people of Israel in the wilderness of Paran, at Kadesh. They brought back word to them and to all the congregation, and showed them the fruit of the land. And they told him, 'We came to the land to which you sent us. It flows with milk and honey, and this is its fruit. *However*, the people who dwell in the land are strong, and the cities are fortified and very large. And besides, we saw the descendants of Anak there'" (Num. 13:25-28).

Irrespective of the land's goodness, the "however" became the majority's emphasis. They saw the glass as half empty. But one can hardly blame them. The odds were stacked against the Israelites big time. As a result, nearly all the spies recommended against fulfilling God's mandate to enter and conquer the Promised Land. Ten of the spies fixated on the enemy's size and strength. They ran the numbers. It was evident that the enemy had them outmatched. But there was one thing they forgot to factor into their decision-making equation: God. They only saw what was humanly possible.

Then, contrary to the naysaying majority, a sole voice called out from the crowd, "Let us go up at once and occupy it, for we are well able to overcome it" (Num. 13:30b). You could have likely heard a pin drop. All eyes were on a man named Caleb, whom God later said had a "different spirit" (see Num. 14:24). Different indeed. What courage to stand with God, but contrary to nearly all of his peers.

Caleb's bravery was then met with immediate pushback from the others.

> "Then the men who had gone up with him said, *'We are not able to go up against the people, for they are stronger than we are.'* So they brought to the people of Israel a bad report of the land that they had spied out, saying, 'The land, through which we have gone to spy it out, is a land that devours its inhabitants, and all the people that we saw in it are of great height. And there we saw the Nephilim (the sons of Anak, who come from the Nephilim), and we seemed to ourselves like grasshoppers, and so we seemed to them'" (Num. 13:31-33).

The ten spies knew what they were up against. They realized that, as the book of Genesis states,

> "The Nephilim were on the earth in those days, and also afterward, when the sons of God came in to the daughters of man and they bore children to them. These were the mighty men who were of old, the men of renown" (Gen. 6:4).

Scripture indicates that "the sons of God" is an Old Testament reference to angels—fallen angels as it pertains to the Nephilim. When cross-referencing Numbers 13:32-33 with Genesis 6:4, we learn that the Nephilim were mixed-race descendants of humans and demons. The New Testament even appears to reference those same demonic beings (in Jude 1:6):

> "And the angels who did not stay within their own position of authority, but left their proper dwelling, he has kept in eternal chains under gloomy darkness until the judgment of the great day."

You see, populating the land of Canaan with the giant Nephilim was Satan's attempt to intimidate God's people and thereby wholly impede God's plans for them. And the devil's strategy almost succeeded.

The thought of a land filled with big, strong giants ready to devour them was psychologically too much for the ten spies to bear. They were persuaded by the *perceived* impossibility of entering—much less occupying—a land with so many "fortified and very large" cities. Gargantuan grapes or not, a gargantuan enemy was all they saw. It wasn't shaping up to be the "all gain, no pain" campaign they may have envisioned.

And so, convinced by the words of the majority, a tide of fear overtook the hearts of all Israel.

Instead of determining to defeat their enemies, Israel was defeated by an invasion of fear before any battle began.

Instead of being confident in God and His impeccable track record, they became convinced that the "Canaan campaign" was doomed to fail.

Instead of standing firm on God's sure promise of victory, they became stuck in the sinking sand of unbelief.

Instead of courageously fighting like victors, they stubbornly assumed the posture of defeated victims.

Any hope of entering the Promised Land was rapidly slipping away. As the people's fear snowballed, it metastasized into anger against Moses, Aaron, and ultimately God Himself.

> "Then all the congregation raised a loud cry, and the people wept that night. And all the people of Israel grumbled against Moses and Aaron. The whole congregation said to them, 'Would that we had died in the land of Egypt! Or would that we had died in this wilderness! Why is the Lord bringing us into this land, to fall by the sword? Our wives and our little ones will become a prey. Would it not be better for us to go back to Egypt? And they said to one another, 'Let us choose a leader and go back to Egypt'" (Num. 14:1-4).

But the situation only continued to deteriorate from there. Anger escalated to outright rage when "all the congregation said to stone them with stones. But the glory of the LORD appeared at the tent of meeting to all the people of Israel" (Num. 14:10). Thankfully, God intervened to stand with the minority who stood for Him.

Instead of simply believing what God could do, the congregation let their human impulses dictate their decisions. At the prospect of fighting spiritual battles against our invisible foe, we can often do the same by allowing fear to burrow its way into our hearts. Especially when the odds are against us, it is easy to believe that nothing will change and things will only worsen. We have all witnessed what appear to be hopeless situations. The Israelites allowed what they saw and heard in the present to prevent them from what God had promised for their future. What they saw eclipsed what they didn't yet see and blinded their eyes from what could be.

Their anger and rage was overt. But there was a more subvert seed that germinated into the outward actions of a mob. What was at the root of all that crazed outrage? Why did all of Israel fight against God instead of taking down the real enemy? Why did the ten spies disagree so sharply with Caleb? One answer: misplaced love. Their fear-driven desire was rooted in idolatrous self-preservation. The intense love of their own lives instinctively kicked back against any stance or person they perceived as "self life" threatening. Fear can only grow in the soil of love for something transient that you know you cannot keep. Caleb's generation opted to barely "get by" in the wilderness than to risk their lives for God. But not Caleb. He realized that, no matter what, the best place to be is where God leads. The safest place to be is in lockstep with Him and His plan.

But without a doubt, Caleb also knew his stance was very unpopular with the people. Like the others, he was well aware of the dangers of fighting fierce warrior giants. Whether at the hands of his "friends" or in the face of the enemy, he knew that the moment he stood up, his life would be at risk. Yet he found courage. But how? Because he cared more about his God than he did his own life. You aren't afraid to lose something that you don't consider yours in the first place. Caleb had armed himself with what Peter wrote about in 1 Peter 4:1-2.

> "Since therefore Christ suffered in the flesh, arm yourselves with the same way of thinking, for whoever has suffered in the flesh has ceased from sin, so as to live for the rest of the time in the flesh no longer for human passions but for the will of God."

Caleb was among those who "did not love their lives so much as to shrink from death" (Rev. 12:11b NIV).

THE POWER OF PROPER PERSPECTIVE

Paul also shared Caleb's perspective. In his second letter to the Corinthians, roughly one and a half millennia later, Paul reminds us that "for we walk by faith, not by sight" (2 Cor. 5:7).

Caleb's faith in God allowed him to see what was yet unseen. No matter how impenetrable the stronghold walls, no matter how big and strong the enemy, Caleb considered something as his, which wasn't yet in his hands. How could Caleb have had such a correct (and counter-cultural) perspective? Because he simply believed that God would deliver on His promise. Like Caleb, when we walk by faith, "we are always of good courage," as Paul wrote just one verse earlier, in 2 Corinthians 5:6.

When we walk by sight, we see how big our enemy is relative to us. When we walk by faith, we see how big our God is relative to our enemy.

Contrary to the narrative "the others" promoted, *with God,* we are not "grasshoppers" or impotent insects under our enemy's feet. "No, in all these things we *are* more than conquerors through Him who loved us" (Rom. 8:37). We "are" currently more than conquerors *now*, not only one day in Heaven.

Friends, it's all a matter of perspective. Our enemy, the devil, is much bigger and stronger than us. But with God (to quote Caleb), "we are well able to overcome" and squash the enemy underfoot because "in the world you will have tribulation. But take heart; I [Jesus] *have* overcome the world" (John 16:33b).[11] Jesus did *not* say, "I *will* overcome the world." He already has overcome the world, past tense.

In the minds of the Israelite majority, the greatness of the giants in the present exceeded the greatness of God eternally.

But only in their minds. As a result of what they already held to, in unbelief, the nation latched onto the words of "the ten." It was as if those words were bricks to build their case for killing the "Canaan campaign" and anyone who backed it.

Rather than attacking the giants that stood in the way of God's plan and promise, the people were ready to throw stones at their friends.

Rather than pulling down fearful thoughts, they elevated mere mindsets and the demons behind them above "He who sits in the heavens" (Ps. 2:4a), above God Himself.

When we aren't "pulling down strongholds, casting down arguments and every high thing that exalts itself against the knowledge of God, bringing every thought into captivity to the obedience of Christ" (2 Cor. 10:4-5 NKJV), we have fallen defeated well before setting foot on any battlefield.

Like Caleb and later Joshua, is God stirring in you to take territory with Him and for Him? But unlike the twelfth century BC Israelites, the enemy we face is predominately unseen. The Lord promised that "every place that the *sole* of" Joshua's "foot will tread upon" (see Josh. 1:3a) would become their territory, His territory. Like Jesus, we have "the feet of those who preach the good news" (Rom. 10:15b) to take unseen territory by setting "at liberty *souls* who are oppressed" (Luke 4:18b).

God has promised to give us territory. But we will take not one square inch of it until we first go and fight against the demonic, the covert captors of souls. We must "tread on serpents and scorpions, and over all the power of the enemy" (see Luke 10:19) in order to take spiritual territory. And as I do and you do, "nothing shall hurt you" (see Luke 10:19). When you act according to Almighty's plan, He will also act. When you move, God will move. He is waiting. He is ready. Are you?

God was asking the Israelites to mature beyond whining in the wilderness into the risks and rigors of war. To battle against enemies from whom they had, to that point, been insulated. Who actually *wants* to do that?! Given a choice, humans naturally opt for what's comfortable—the path of least resistance—over something that requires real courage.

If you don't want to fight the spiritual battles God is calling you to, you are doing what is natural and normal. You are doing the "sensible" thing. But just sticking to the status quo wasn't enough for Caleb. He knew that he was meant for more. He knew he was equipped for more because he knew the "God of more." He knew that, easy or not, coming up against any enemy weaker than God makes perfect sense.

Caleb acted in faith, faith in a God he considered more powerful than any "strong" giant. He realized that there is no enemy that its Creator cannot overpower.

THE PATH OF PROPER PERSPECTIVE

Today, if you are afraid or unwilling to do that "next thing" the Holy Spirit is asking of you, it might be because you're looking at the wrong things.

Have you lost sight of Jesus? Have you let what you see eclipse what you can't see? If so, it might be time for a better perspective, a higher perspective. God's perspective. Whenever we see any giant as *big*, we perceive God as *little* in comparison. In truth, "big God, little giants" is the only reality.

Inspired by Caleb's stand-alone faith, just one chapter later (in Numbers 14:6-9), Joshua found the strength to join Caleb to stand for God.

> "And Joshua the son of Nun and Caleb the son of Jephunneh, who were among those who had spied out the land, tore their clothes and said to all the congregation of the people of Israel, "The land, which we passed through to spy it out, is an exceedingly good land. If the LORD delights in us, he will bring us into this land and give it to us, a land that flows with milk and honey. Only do not rebel against the LORD. And do not fear the people of the land, for they are bread for us. Their protection is removed from them, and the LORD is with us; do not fear them."

Caleb and Joshua were different from the others. They were the oddballs, but they were nevertheless in tune with the Lord.

And it was that proper divine perspective that dictated their proper path. God affirmed Caleb by stating, "because my servant Caleb has a different spirit and follows me wholeheartedly, I will bring him into the land he went to, and his descendants will inherit it" (Num. 14:24 NIV).

Still today, those who undertake daring deeds of faith for the Lord are few. They are the outliers. It is more common to lament one's problems rather than see things from God's viewpoint and overcome them. It is more typical *not* to trust the Lord and, as a result, live lives of defeat. Many prefer fearing for their lives rather than living fearless lives that matter.

But the time has come for courage and confidence in the Lord to become the norm among Christians everywhere. Now is the time to take God at His word, motivated to see His "kingdom come, [His] will be done, on earth as it is in heaven" (see Matt. 6:10).[12] Today is the day to stop letting the enemy intimidate us into inaction. God is ready to raise up a people who refuse to settle for the way things have been. He is looking for those unsatisfied with anything less than what He is eager to do now.

"The eyes of the LORD search the whole earth in order to strengthen those whose hearts are fully committed to him" (2 Chron. 16:9a NLT). Are you fully committed to God even when you can't see what's next? Joshua was, and it was astounding what God did through just that one individual. Fast-forward one generation to the book of Joshua.

CHAPTER 4

BE CAREFUL

"Only be strong and very courageous, being careful to do according to all the law that Moses my servant commanded you. Do not turn from it to the right hand or to the left, that you may have good success wherever you go."

JOSHUA 1:7

Things looked bleak for the people of Israel. Moses was dead. The generation who heeded the word of the ten spies, over the word of God, died in the desert without setting foot in the Promised Land. Instead of taking territory from the enemy, all of Caleb's fellow compatriots were literally defeated by fear. Tragically, fear kept them from fighting battles God had assured them of winning (see Josh. 3:10-11). The only battles they ever fought and lost were in their heads. The author of Hebrews wrote this about that unbelieving generation (3:16-19):

"For who were those who heard and yet rebelled? Was it not all those who left Egypt led by Moses? And with whom was he provoked for forty years? Was it not with those who sinned, whose bodies fell in the wilderness? And to whom did he swear that they would not enter his rest, but to those who were disobedient? So we see that they were unable to enter because of unbelief."

TAKE CARE, TAKE TERRITORY

Instead of leaving a legacy of strong faith, Moses' generation left enemy strongholds to their children—strongholds they should have defeated for their children and grandchildren. *But a new era was dawning,* an age of faith and victory. It was time for the faithful to fight! As Joshua stood on the border of the Promised Land, God restated His commission, His mandate, to arise and go!

> "After the death of Moses the servant of the LORD, the LORD said to Joshua the son of Nun, Moses' assistant, 'Moses my servant is dead. Now therefore arise, go over this Jordan, you and all this people, into the land that I am giving to them, to the people of Israel'" (Josh. 1:1-2).

Then, the Lord followed this mandate with a promise. In the next three verses (1:3-5), He assured Joshua that,

> "Every place that the sole of your foot will tread upon I have given to you, just as I promised to Moses. From the wilderness and this Lebanon as far as the great river, the river Euphrates, all the land of the Hittites to the Great

Sea toward the going down of the sun shall be your territory. No man shall be able to stand before you all the days of your life. Just as I was with Moses, so I will be with you. I will not leave you or forsake you."

Notice God's words, "Just as I was with Moses, so I will be with you. I will not leave you or forsake you" (Josh. 1:5b). Thankfully, the mandate to war also came with the Man of War (see Exod. 15:3 NKJV). God Himself was the essential "it" factor. As Paul rhetorically wrote to the Romans: "If God is for us, who can be against us?" (Rom. 8:31b). The Almighty is the ultimate ally.

If the Lord's presence is the power for victory, following His lead is the strategic path to victory. Like any successful military engagement, superior strength and strategy are both necessary.

Read on in Joshua 1:6-8,

> "Be strong and courageous, for you shall cause this people to inherit the land that I swore to their fathers to give them. Only be strong and very courageous, being careful to do according to all the law that Moses my servant commanded you. Do not turn from it to the right hand or to the left, that you may have good success wherever you go. This Book of the Law shall not depart from your mouth, but you shall meditate on it day and night, so that you may be careful to do according to all that is

written in it. For then you will make your way prosperous, and then you will have good success."

How can we have the courage to fight for the Lord like Joshua did, as Caleb did? Reread the first half of verse 7: "Only be strong and very courageous, *being careful to do according to all the law that Moses my servant commanded you.*"

When we are careful to live right privately before God, we will have the courage to do what is right publicly before others. Personal, private obedience to God is what builds public boldness for Him. Joshua knew this. As God stated in the second half of Joshua 1:7, "Do not turn from it to the right hand or to the left, *that you may have good success wherever you go.*" It is, therefore, no surprise that Joshua later said to the people (*before* going to battle), "Consecrate yourselves, for tomorrow the Lord will do wonders among you" (Josh. 3:5b). Consecration to God must come before spiritual "conquering" for God.

Nothing will zap your will to fight for God quicker than compromising sin. And preferring any sin over the Savior always invites demons. Therefore, we should regularly pray, "Search me, O God, and know my heart; Try me, and know my anxieties; And see if there is any wicked way in me, And lead me in the way everlasting" (Ps. 139:23-24 NKJV). Proverbs 28:1 is clear that "the wicked flee when no one pursues, but the righteous are bold as a lion." Isaiah referred to another type of lion from whom those who walk in "the Way of Holiness" will be protected (see Isa. 35:8). He wrote,

"No lion shall be there, nor shall any ravenous beast come up on it; they shall not be found there, but the redeemed shall walk there" (Isa. 35:9).

When you walk in integrity, purity, and righteousness before the Lord, the Lord stands ready to fight with you. He *Himself* will be your shield—as He was to Abram, to whom He said, "Do not be afraid, Abram. *I am your shield*, your very great reward" (Gen. 15:1 NIV). The believer's shield does *not* consist of metal, wood, or any other material—it is instead the embodiment of God Himself. This truth is echoed throughout Scripture. Proverbs 2:7-8 states,

> "He [the Lord] stores up sound wisdom for the upright; *he is a shield to those who walk in integrity*, guarding the paths of justice and watching over the way of his saints."[13]

When we sin, if we confess that sin, draw near to God, and submit to Him, He will help us. "And if anyone sins, we have an Advocate with the Father, Jesus Christ the righteous" (1 John 2:1b NKJV). When you run to God for help, He will rush in with His strength to empower you to "resist the devil" so that "he will flee from you" (see James 4:7). When you "put on the whole armor of God" (Eph. 6:11a), you will be armed to push back the enemy powerfully.

But conversely, if we resist God, He will resist us. As James wrote (4:6 NKJV) to his fellow Christian brothers and sisters,

> "But He gives more grace. Therefore He says: 'God resists the proud, But gives grace to the humble.'"

Although God promises to "never leave you nor forsake you" (Heb. 13:5b), when it comes to our daily spiritual battles, the biblical relevance behind what the Spirit spoke to Judean King Asa thousands of years ago still applies today:

> "The LORD is with you *while you are with him*. If you seek him, he will be found by you, but if you forsake him, he will forsake you" (2 Chron. 15:2b).

God will never force any person to be "with Him." But going it alone without the Lord is the epitome of pride and the equivalent of resisting God. We can either partner with the author of pride (the devil) or else follow Joshua's and Jesus's examples of humble submission to the Father.

TAKE COURAGE, TAKE TERRITORY

Despite the fact that we, as Christian believers, live in a physical world, "For we are *not* fighting against flesh-and-blood enemies, but against evil rulers and authorities of the *unseen world*, against mighty powers in this dark world, and *against evil spirits in the heavenly places*" (Eph. 6:12 NLT). "We are human, but *we don't wage war as humans do*. We use God's mighty weapons, *not worldly weapons*, to knock down the strongholds of human reasoning and to destroy false arguments" (2 Cor. 10:4-5 NLT). We have the great privilege of bringing "the gospel of peace" even to those who are battling against the One who "himself is our peace" (see Eph. 6:15; 2:14).

Even though God has *not* called us to war against people (see Matt. 26:51-53; Eph. 6:12), we can nevertheless glean parallel warfare principles from Joshua about how we can wage spiritual battle against *unseen* evil forces.

As in Joshua's time, any time is an excellent time to seek God's help, to "let the weak say, 'I am a warrior'" (Joel 3:10b).

As in Joshua's time, we are also called to fight in faith against a mortal enemy.

As in Joshua's time, there are still strongholds to demolish.

As in Joshua's time, we have a mission as God's people.

As in Joshua's time, those who have a "different spirit" by believing in God's promises can conquer much territory for God's Kingdom.

As in Joshua's time, many still doubt what God can do. But thankfully, "For whatever was written in former days was written for our instruction, that through endurance and through the encouragement of the Scriptures we might have hope" (Rom. 15:4).

As in Joshua's time, we will lose battles when we have unrepentant sin and unfruitfulness in our lives (compare Josh. 7:1-26 to 1 Cor. 11:27-32 and 2 Pet. 1:5-10).

As in Joshua's time, we can only secure victory in the exploits of God if we are "careful" to follow His lead. But to follow Him, we must first learn to listen to His voice. In John 10:27, Jesus said, "My sheep *hear my voice*, and I know them, and *they follow me*." Practical daily victories hinge on hearing and heeding God's voice.

This is what the Lord spoke to King Saul in 1 Samuel 15:22.

> "And Samuel said, 'Has the LORD as great delight in burnt offerings and sacrifices, as in *obeying the voice of the LORD*? Behold, to obey is better than sacrifice, and to listen than the fat of rams.'"

Unlike Saul, whom God later rejected as King due to his disobedience, Joshua was attentive to his Lord's voice. He understood the importance of listening and following, even when he didn't understand what was next. He exemplified Proverbs 3:5, which says to "trust in the LORD with all your heart, and *do not* lean on your own understanding."

When the Lord told Joshua to "go over this Jordan, you and all this people" (see Josh. 1:2), Joshua could have retorted, "But how am I supposed to get an entire nation across such a wide and deep river? Where's the bridge? That's impossible." He could have put conditions on obedience: "God, before I do anything, you first need to share the battle plan with me. You tell me to go, but you haven't told me how we will win." If you re-read the first few verses of Joshua 1, you will notice that God never provided Joshua with a battle plan. He just said, "go."

Strange though it may seem to some, it has always been God's style to reveal one step at a time and not always explain Himself. That is how He first called Abraham (formerly Abram) to go "to the land that I *will* show you," future tense (Gen. 12:1b). The Lord revealed each next step to Abraham during his daily walk with God. Hebrews 11:8 further clarifies with these words, "By faith Abraham obeyed when he was called to go out to a place that he was to receive as an inheritance. And he went out, *not knowing where he was going.*"

Thousands of years after He initially called Abraham, we still see God working in the same manner. Like when Jesus asked Peter to cast his nets "into the deep" and later "on the right side of the boat" (see Luke 5:4; John 21:6). Although he didn't see the logic in Jesus's requests (he had literally already been there, done that), Peter still responded, "But at your word I will let down the nets" (Luke 5:5b). There was no special formula that yielded success for that first-century fisherman. Instead, what made all the difference is what always makes all the difference: simply following the lead Fisherman. We cannot formulate or fabricate what *God* wants to do because it's "'Not by might nor by power, but by my Spirit,' says the Lord Almighty" (Zech. 4:6b NIV).

How God led and worked with Abraham, Joshua, and Peter was not exclusive to them. It is the norm in His Kingdom.

Jesus said, "The kingdom of God is as if a man should scatter seed on the ground. He sleeps and rises night and day, and the seed sprouts and grows; *he knows not how*" (Mark 4:26-27). God plans, works, and wars in advance to a level of detail that we don't always understand or see. But simply because we don't comprehend how the Lord will work something out doesn't mean He won't. Us *not* knowing what only God knows never justifies us not following where God leads.

In response to the Lord's call to lead Israel across the Jordan, Joshua responded as his forefather Abraham did—in simple obedience. See Joshua 1:10-11.

> "And Joshua commanded the officers of the people, 'Pass through the midst of the camp and command the people, 'Prepare your provisions, for within three days you are to pass over this Jordan to go in to take possession of the land that the LORD your God is giving you to possess.'"

Joshua authenticated his trust in God by the action of leading others into what God had called him and them to do. The book of Joshua is a biography of a man who didn't just "make something up" but instead listened up, looked up, and got up to follow God's lead. Joshua navigated the nuances and challenges he faced by staying in step with God every step of the way, day by day, battle after battle. He realized something: knowing God is our battle plan. "The people who know their God will be strong and take action" (Dan. 11:32b NASB).

Now is a good point for me to attempt to clear up something. Contrary to what has been promulgated in some songs and Christian circles, crossing the Jordan river into the Promised Land of Canaan did *not* symbolize entering Heaven. How do I know that? One only has to read the first 12 chapters of Joshua to realize that Canaan was no Heaven. Flowing with "milk and honey" or not, the land God promised Israel was unobtainable without intense battles. Will there be any enemies or battles in Heaven? No, of course not. Joshua fought many battles against Israel's enemies. Is faith needed in Heaven? No, because on that day, our "faith shall be sight," as a famous hymn writer once put it[14] (consistent with Revelation 7). Joshua had to walk by faith every step of the way while in Canaan. Will there be enemy territory to take in Heaven? No, Heaven is already 100% God's territory.

What then does unconquered Canaan symbolize? It represents all human souls enslaved by sin and controlled by "the prince of the power of the air, the spirit who now works in the sons of disobedience" (Eph. 2:2b NKJV). Will you and I be among the courageous Christians who take back spiritual territory with the Prince of Peace (see Isa. 9:6), the perfect Joshua (Jeshua or Jesus), at our side? Will we assume our Christ-ordained "ministry" as "ambassadors for Christ, as though God were pleading through us" (see 2 Cor. 5:18-20 NKJV) to courageously rescue others, like He has done for us, "from the power of darkness and conveyed us into the kingdom of the Son of His love" (Col. 1:13b NKJV)? Or will we come to the end of our days only to have lived in a wilderness of self-inflicted defeat like Moses' generation?

We can whine against God and others. Or we can war against the enemy and for others.

We can lament the pervasive problems of earth. Or we can do something about them by calling down the powerful solutions of Heaven until we see the earth "filled with the knowledge of the glory of the Lord as the waters cover the sea" (see Hab. 2:14).

We can complain about the territory that the devil currently controls. Or we can boldly take back what rightfully belongs to our God.

We can cower in fear. Or we can be strong and courageous.

CHAPTER 5

BE STRONG

"Have I not commanded you? Be strong and courageous. Do not be frightened, and do not be dismayed, for the LORD your God is with you wherever you go."

JOSHUA 1:9

Many people can relate to being bullied in one form or another, especially in their younger years. Some of my classmates likewise bullied me as a boy. With no provocation on my part, there was no apparent reason why they targeted me. I now realize that another (unseen) bully was at work behind the scenes. Although his intimidation tactics often take different forms, the devil *tries* to intimidate and "train" each of us to assume the posture of fearful victims instead of courageous spiritual victors who resist him.

Upon entering the Promised Land, the enemies of God projected their fear onto Joshua. God encouraged Joshua (in Josh.

1:9) to "not be frightened." But we learn just one chapter later (in Joshua 2:9-11) that God's enemies ironically "melted" with terror. As Rahab revealed to the spies:

> "I know that the LORD has given you the land, and that the fear of you has fallen upon us, and that all the inhabitants of the land melt away before you. For we have heard how the LORD dried up the water of the Red Sea before you when you came out of Egypt, and what you did to the two kings of the Amorites who were beyond the Jordan, to Sihon and Og, whom you devoted to destruction. And as soon as we heard it, *our hearts melted, and there was no spirit left in any man because of you, for the LORD your God, he is God in the heavens above and on the earth beneath.*"

Despite being "safe" within the stronghold of Jericho, the enemy knew it was powerless to stand against anyone who stood with Almighty God.

There is a secret your adversary *doesn't* want you to know: Satan is more afraid of you than you are of him because he knows Who is with you. As 1 John 4:4b (NKJV) affirms, "He who is in you is greater than he who is in the world." The enemy cunningly tries to intimidate us because he is intimidated by the One in us.

On the other hand, any believer who tries to fight apart from God's leading, apart from God, will be beaten by our unseen bully (the devil) every time. David acknowledged in Psalm 18:17 that only God can rescue "from my strong enemy and from those who hated me, for they were too mighty for me." No matter what comes your way, the enemy is no match for your Dad. The more closely you are in step with the Father, the more you threaten your adversary.

It is, therefore, no surprise that great demonic fear often tries to creep in when we are attempting great feats for the Kingdom. At their core, all such affronts are attempts to wedge us away from our strong God. The devil is acutely aware of what Jesus asserted: "without Me you can do *nothing*" (John 15:5b NKJV). The enemy knows that, if left unchecked, fear will restrain us from reaching out to our heavenly lifeline, to God. But we must remember that any fear we experience as God's children is entirely unfounded. Fear is nothing more than Satanic smoke and mirrors meant to obscure our view of our Father. My wife often says, "we are not called to worry, but to war." Instead of cowering, it's time to take the fight to the enemy. That's what Joshua did.

That said, don't assume for a moment that simply because he pushed forward in faith, Joshua didn't first feel fear. He did, but he didn't let that fear control him. Fear *will* come. It comes to everyone. Fear may come as you attempt to conquer what darkness controls; it comes with that (spiritual) territory. The enemy may appear terrifying when left unchallenged. But the reality is that "The light shines in the darkness, and the darkness can never extinguish it" (John 1:5 NLT).

Each time you step into courage, a strong warrior's heart will arise in you, at which point, Satan won't seem as scary, if at all.

Fear can either be a curse that cripples or a catalyst that emboldens courage. When fear comes, you will conquer it or be conquered by it.

As quickly as the feelings of fear came to Joshua, God also came to remind him of what He said to all of Israel back in Deuteronomy 7, verses 18 and 21 (NKJV): "You shall not be afraid of them, but you shall remember well what the LORD your God did to Pharaoh and to all Egypt" and "You shall not be terrified of them; for the LORD your God, the great and awesome God, is among you." God personalized that encouragement to Joshua when He reminded him of His command by saying,

> "Have I not commanded you? Be strong and courageous. Do not be frightened, and do not be dismayed, *for the LORD your God is with you wherever you go*" (Josh. 1:9).

"I am with you" was God's faith-building encouragement to be strong. The way to "be strong" is "in the Lord and in the strength of His might" (see Eph. 6:10). The source of your strength is singular. We cannot take one inch of territory for the Kingdom without the King coming with us. Going *with* God was, and still is, the secret to conquering fear and overpowering the enemy. This same principle underpins what Jesus said in John 15:5b: "apart from me you can do *nothing*."

To quote King David, "The LORD is the strength of my life" (see Ps. 27:1 NKJV). Samuel recorded (in 2 Samuel 8:6b) that "the LORD gave victory to David wherever he went." But David only realized those victories because he first recognized his need to seek God's guidance. Directly following David's coronation in 2 Samuel 5, his long-time enemy came to war against him. What did David do upon hearing such news?

> "And *David inquired of the LORD*, 'Shall I go up against the Philistines? Will you give them into my hand?' And the LORD said to David, 'Go up, for I will certainly give the Philistines into your hand.' And David came to Baal-perazim, and David defeated them there'" (2 Sam. 5:19-20a).

Before acting, David first asked.

Then, only a few verses later, we learn that "And the Philistines came up *yet again* and spread out in the Valley of Rephaim" (2 Sam. 5:22). But yet again, David asked the Lord what to do. It was good that he did because the plan for the second battle was different from the first.

> "And when David inquired of the LORD, he said, 'You shall not go up; go around to their rear, and come against them opposite the balsam trees. And when you hear the sound of marching in the tops of the balsam trees, then rouse yourself, for then the LORD has gone out before you to strike down the army of the Philistines.' And David

did as the LORD commanded him, and struck down the Philistines from Geba to Gezer" (2 Sam. 5:23-25).

How were saints like Joshua and David able to obey the moment God said it was "go time"? Those decisions were *only* possible because of all the moments that led up to them. Like David, Joshua's strong relationship with God did not magically materialize in a day. It was forged throughout all the years prior.

Joshua was prepared to encounter the enemy *only* because he first encountered his God. He cultivated a personal culture of approaching God well before approaching the Canaanite border. The moment of battle victory was built upon all the moments (plural) that built up to it. Before the battle, there was a backstory. A passage in Exodus 33:7-11 gives us a glimpse into Joshua's personal culture of worship and intimacy with God.

> "Now Moses used to take the tent and pitch it outside the camp, far off from the camp, and he called it the tent of meeting. And everyone who sought the LORD would go out to the tent of meeting, which was outside the camp. Whenever Moses went out to the tent, all the people would rise up, and each would stand at his tent door, and watch Moses until he had gone into the tent. When Moses entered the tent, the pillar of cloud would descend and stand at the entrance of the tent, and the LORD would speak with Moses. And when all the people

saw the pillar of cloud standing at the entrance of the tent, all the people would rise up and worship, each at his tent door. Thus the LORD used to speak to Moses face to face, as a man speaks to his friend. *When Moses turned again into the camp, his assistant Joshua the son of Nun, a young man, would not depart from the tent."*

Notice that Joshua was not content to merely admire Moses' relationship with God. Observing God from afar like the rest of Israel was not enough for him. No, Joshua had to have God for himself, personally. Even after leader Moses left God's presence, Joshua still lingered there. Joshua did not allow himself to be limited even by his spiritual leader. The duration of Moses' time with God wasn't even enough for Joshua. He had to have more. Even "when Moses turned again into the camp, his assistant Joshua the son of Nun, a young man, would not depart from the tent" (Exod. 33:11). Joshua understood the incomparable value and joy of pausing and persisting in God's presence.

Singing songs from the comfort of his tent wasn't enough, even if it was what everyone else did. Joshua didn't mind the inconvenience of going out or even the ridicule of standing out, as long as it meant he got to draw near to his God. He dwelt among a generation that was supposed to believe God but didn't. Instead of conforming to a collective "camp," *nominal* Israel in his case, Joshua chose to identify with God. Instead of being loyal to the prevailing patterns of a wayward people group, Joshua was determined to find his way to God, even if it meant meeting Him outside the city. According to Hebrews 13:12-15, we should do the same:

> "So Jesus also suffered outside the gate in order to sanctify the people through his own blood. *Therefore let us go to him outside the camp and bear the reproach he endured. For here we have no lasting city*, but we seek the city that is to come. Through him then *let us continually offer up a sacrifice of praise to God*, that is, the fruit of lips that acknowledge his name."

Instead of considering any human-made place or person his home, Joshua (like Abraham) "was looking forward to the city that has foundations, whose designer and builder is God" (Heb. 11:10).

Joshua's bravery in the latter battles of Canaan was forged by his former willingness to enter into God's presence even when others could care less. He developed fortitude by worshiping God even while his generation whined against God.

When we worship the Father in spirit and truth, we expose demonic facades and demolish fabrications that Satan is stronger than the Almighty. By lifting his eyes to his God, Joshua was strengthened and trained to look past what the enemy was doing to what God was about to do.

But again, even though Joshua was able to "carry out great exploits" for God as he walked with God (see Dan. 11:32 NKJV), doing so came with counter-attacks from the devil. The same is still a reality today. The enemy will never quit coming to hound you and me. He will never give up coming against us. Like Joshua, this is why we must keep going to our all-strong God. And as we do, we must boldly speak all that we hear the Father saying and live out all we see Him doing. No matter how seemingly impossible, we are to faithfully walk in the works God has prepared beforehand for us to walk in (see Eph. 2:10).

God honored His promise and Joshua's faith by miraculously parting the Jordan river and later winning battles despite impossible odds. When Joshua walked with God, God walked with him. When Joshua simply listened and followed his High Commander, the Lord masterfully managed all the battle complexity on behalf of His people. But the miracles only manifested when faith grew feet, as in Joshua 3:15b-16a when "the feet of the priests bearing the ark were dipped in the brink of the water (now the Jordan overflows all its banks throughout the time of harvest), the waters coming down from above stood and rose up in a heap very far away."

When Jesus says to "go," just go. When He says "wait," be patient and wait. When He says "do this" or "say that," just "trust and obey."[15]

The One who goes with you also wants to go before you. Jesus is well able to overcome any fear that overwhelms you because He is King over everything.

It's time to be aware, be awake, be believing, be careful, and "finally, be strong in the Lord and in the strength of His might" (Eph. 6:10 NASB).

It's time to turn the tables on the enemy because he is far more terrified of the One who lives in you than you are of him.

But dealing with demonic fear is only phase one of dealing blows to the enemy. The next step involves getting up even when you feel like staying down.

PART 2

CRUSHING DISCOURAGEMENT

It's time to take courage from above

CHAPTER 6

DISCOURAGEMENT INCAPACITATES

"For we do not want you to be unaware, brothers, of the affliction we experienced in Asia. For we were so utterly burdened beyond our strength that we despaired of life itself."

2 CORINTHIANS 1:8

One-on-one ministry can be life-changing. There is something one-of-a-kind about spending one-on-one time with someone unique from hanging out in a group setting. As prompted by the Holy Spirit, I often share breakfast, lunch, or coffee with other guys. On a particular occasion, I had a meal with a man facing some challenges in his life. As we ate, I listened, but I also conveyed Jesus's love with my countenance and words.

As I have experienced on many occasions, I sensed the Father looking at the person across the table from me through my eyes. I saw the Father loving him through me. I could sense an unseen transaction, a deposit, taking place. The Father was imparting something of Himself to that individual. As I usually do, I prayed for him before and after we met. And as I often later learn, that man's discouraged heart and outlook on life had been significantly lifted due to our time together.

Just one Spirit-led act of kindness. Just one shared meal and someone's life was impacted. Not surprisingly, ministering over a meal was one of Jesus's favorite forms of expressing God's love. Jesus was especially fond of eating with those others overlooked—even if it meant He became the brunt of ridicule by the religious elite (see Matt. 9:9-13).

It is easy to underestimate the life-altering power of even one encounter with the Father's love. I am *not* a licensed counselor, but the "Wonderful Counselor" lives in me (see Isa. 9:6; 1 Cor. 3:16). He lives in you, too, if you love Jesus (see John 14:23-28).

TOO DOWN TO GET UP

Getting up to resist the devil is the last thing I want to do when I feel down. Maybe you can relate. While writing this book, the enemy regularly pounded me with waves of discouragement. My mind was often crippled with mental confusion for no explainable reason. At times, the resistance from the enemy was so intense that it took hours to fight through the attack. But like a boxer who refuses to give up, the harder I got hit, the more skilled I became at striking back. The more rapidly the attack came, the quicker and more fervently I sought God's help.

There were instances when my mind was so overwhelmed and my heart so downcast, that all I could initially do was simply worship in song. Like King Jehoshaphat, praise led the charge against the enemy[16] in the sentiment, "We do not know what to do, but our eyes are on you" (2 Chron. 20:12b). I poured out my heart in prayer to my Father (see Ps. 62:8). The Holy Spirit often instructed me from a Scripture passage specific to my situation (see 1 John 2:27). Like Jesus, I then commanded the enemy to flee from me (see Matt. 4:10). Regardless of the nature of the attack, every time "the flaming darts" (see Eph. 6:16) were fired at me, God delivered me. Time and again, He picked me up so I could push back and pick up my proverbial pen.

I recall a particularly long night of discouragement. I arose early the following day to seek the Lord. But "even before a word is on my tongue" (Ps. 139:4a), before I could confess my lack of trust in Him, I heard the Father interrupt me to say, "I love you son." Tears began to flow as my heart melted in the presence of Love Himself. I sat, then stood, cried, prayed, sang, and danced for the next hour. Being with the Lord "turned for me my mourning into dancing" (Ps. 30:11a). No matter what I go through, I always experience the deliverance and encouragement of the Lord. Thanks to my faithful Father, a *dis*couraged heart *always* gives way to an *en*couraged heart.

Like me, without courage, you cannot fight. Without courage, you will not fight. Without courage, it will be okay by you to be bullied by the devil, by the "discourager."

TIME TO GIVE UP?

Do you ever feel like giving up? Perhaps you've been knocked down so many times that you would rather just lay down and stay down. Maybe you are even starting to believe that that is where you belong. Or perhaps you are afraid of what will happen if you fight back and go "all in" to trust God and resist the devil.

If you've been discouraged, you're not alone. If you ever feel bad, you're in good company. Even Paul, the most prolific New Testament author and outspoken first century AD ambassador for Christ, endured extreme emotional pain. Especially while working for the Lord, Paul experienced despair, sleeplessness, anxiety, and "daily pressure"—among "other things" (see 2 Cor. 1:8, 11:27-28; Phil. 2:28).

The apostle Paul wasn't superhuman despite how some Bible teachers portray him. Nor did he hide his weakness and struggles from others; he was very transparent. Paul shamelessly expressed the despair that he endured when he wrote, "For we do not want you to be unaware, brothers, of the affliction we experienced in Asia. For we were *so utterly burdened beyond our strength that we despaired of life itself*" (2 Cor. 1:8). At times life was so difficult that Paul "despaired of life itself."

That's some heavy discouragement. But even though he was authentic about his afflictions, Paul didn't let those burdens bog him down. He instead affirmed his trust in God by testifying to His track record of deliverance while declaring the same for the future. In 2 Corinthians 1:10, Paul penned this:

> "*He delivered us* from such a deadly peril, and *he will deliver us*. On him we have set our hope that *he will deliver us again.*"

Our words unhide what's in our hearts. Irrespective of our feelings, our speech either confirms or denies our faith in God (see Luke 6:45).

Like Paul, the writers of the Psalms also regularly expressed their discouragement. But, even while life was hard, those same psalmists always worshiped God for the encouragement they had yet to experience in His presence. They turned from looking down at their pain to looking up in praise to God. The writer of Psalm 42:11 exemplified this when he talked to himself and told his troubled soul to praise God: "Why are you in despair, my soul? And why are you restless within me? Wait for God, for I will again praise Him For the help of His presence, my God" (Ps. 42:11 NASB).

Especially during such dark days, I would be hard-pressed to overstate the importance of encouragement. Perhaps you are thinking, "Encouragement... why devote an entire section of the book to that?!" Many often confuse encouragement with flattery or fake positivity. That's not at all what I'm talking about. Flattery is just falsehood disguised as friendship. Puffery should have no place among God's people. But real discouragement requires real encouragement, the kind that ultimately flows from God to you.

TIME TO GET UP!

When you "hit a wall," is your natural reaction to focus on the wall? Well, God's encouragement is what keeps us going even when we encounter roadblocks. Godly encouragement is the essential but often absent agent needed to crush discouragement.

When was the last time someone encouraged you? If encouragement is the antidote to discouragement, why don't more Christians encourage others? I fear that it's often because others have told us too much encouragement is dangerous. After all, we don't want to give anyone a "big head." But is that line of thinking in line with how God thinks?

Paul said to "earnestly desire the spiritual gifts, especially that you may prophesy," and "the one who prophesies speaks to people *for their upbuilding and encouragement and consolation*" (1 Cor. 14:1b, 3b). Even though some evangelicals de-prioritize prophecy, God tells us to desire it more than any other spiritual gift. Why? Because the byproduct of prophecy is courage. Courage to fight the good fight. When we prophesy, we give courage, we *en*courage. Case in point, Paul wrote,

> "This charge I entrust to you, Timothy, my child, *in accordance with the prophecies previously made about you, that by them you may wage the good warfare*" (1 Tim. 1:18).

Despite it being essential for winning spiritual battles, there are still some who nevertheless despise prophecy. But to do so is to toss a wet blanket on what is burning in God's heart. Ignoring or even downplaying legitimate, love-motivated prophecy quenches the very work of God. By the Spirit, Paul pointedly said, "Do not quench the Spirit. Do not despise prophecies" (1 Thess. 5:19-20).

God has always taken encouragement very seriously. He is the original Encourager. The original Prophet. He invented encouragement. Encouragement is His original idea, not ours. In Romans 15:5, Paul refers to our Father as "the God of endurance and encouragement." God is the one who first came to encourage us when we were discouraged and without hope.

The people and circumstances that surround us will inevitably discourage us. It has already happened and will happen again and again. Just expect it. But if we are not careful, our discouragement can birth bitterness toward the people who disappoint us. Or worse, toward God, whom many mistakenly think has let them down. Unforgiveness ruins you and others (see Heb. 12:15). Bitterness blinds us to Satan's schemes. Paul affirmed that reality to the Corinthians when he said,

> "Anyone whom you forgive, I also forgive. Indeed, what I have forgiven, if I have forgiven anything, has been

for your sake in the presence of Christ, so *that we would not be outwitted by Satan; for we are not ignorant of his designs*" (2 Cor. 2:10-11).

Nothing enables the evil one to trick us into being his puppet rag dolls more than unforgiveness. Whenever we refuse to forgive anyone who has wronged us, we put out a welcome mat for the devil. According to Jesus's *Parable of the Unforgiving Servant* (see Matt. 18:21-35), unforgiveness invites "tormentors" into our lives (see Matt. 18:34 KJV). When we remain embittered against someone, we empower Satan to fight through us against decoys (other people) rather than against him, our only real enemy.

Although others might consider you their enemy, Jesus's mandate is to love and pray for everyone… even those who may hate you (see Matt. 5:38-48). Paul wrote to his fellow believers in Ephesus: "'In your anger do not sin': Do not let the sun go down while you are still angry, and do not give the devil a foothold" (Eph. 4:26-27 NIV). In the Lord's Prayer, it is no accident that Jesus followed "and forgive us our debts, as we forgive our debtors" with "and do not lead us into temptation, but deliver us from the evil one" (Matt. 6:12, 13a NKJV). Based on the NKJV translation, about 1/3 of the words in Jesus's 66-word model prayer pertain to the importance of forgiveness (for ourselves and others).[17]

Unforgiveness is the antithesis of love. The temptation to be unforgiving and unloving is one we must fight against at all costs. It's time to retaliate against our only real enemy as we forgive and fight for people. It's time to lay down the old and worthless weapons of the flesh. Those *aren't* our weapons, "For the weapons of *our* warfare are *not of the flesh* but have divine power to destroy strongholds" (2 Cor. 10:4).

When you are heavily burdened by what you face, you face a choice. You can let bitterness (or any other sin) set you back. Or you can instead "be strengthened by the grace that is in Christ Jesus" (2 Tim. 2:1b). You can quickly receive and then move on to share the forgiveness offered by your Father of freedom. Or you can dwell in disappointment because of who (or what) has let you down, even if that "who" is you. That's easy to do but also the worst thing you can do. The longer you stew on something, the more sway it will have over you; the more important and influential that thing becomes, *in your estimation.* It starts at a subconscious level and then spreads from there. The longer you "look" at something, good or bad, the more you will magnify it in your mind and manifest it in your life. What has captivated your attention? What has preoccupied your thoughts?

What did Paul prescribe for a bummed brain? While on house arrest, he could have meditated on his horrible circumstances. But that's *not* what he did. Instead, he decided to encourage other believers by entreating them to "rejoice in the Lord always," to "in everything by prayer and supplication with thanksgiving let your requests be made known to God," and finally, "whatever is true, whatever is honorable, whatever is just, whatever is pure, whatever is lovely, whatever is commendable, if there is any excellence, if there is anything worthy of praise, think about these things" (Phil. 4:4a, 6b, 8).

Even when they persist, worthless thoughts do not deserve your attention. But the Lord does. Jesus is the only "true" one. There is none more "honorable" than Him. God will always be perfectly "just" and the only One who is "pure." No one is as "lovely," "commendable," excellent, and "worthy of praise" as Him. I believe that the implied common thread of the "good thoughts list" of Philippians 4:8 is the person of Jesus; who He is (His character), what He has done (His testimony) and will do (His promises), and what He otherwise says (His words). When we boil down what we should be thinking about, we get one thing, one Someone more than anyone: Jesus. Who better to dwell on than the One who will never disappoint?! Who else will we always have reason to rejoice than in the One with "the name that is above every name" (Phil. 2:9b)?! The next time you catch yourself thinking about anything that causes mental turmoil, it's time to start praising, praying, and thinking about Jesus.

Meditate more on the Master and less on any other "high thing that exalts itself against the knowledge of God" (2 Cor. 10:5a). Guess what? You can only think about one thing at a time. Isaiah (26:3) recognized this reality when he wrote about what God does for those who trust Him: "You keep him in perfect peace *whose mind is stayed on you*, because he trusts in you."

It's time to dump demonic discouragement like you would any toxic relationship. Don't let it hang around anymore; it only wants to use and abuse you. It's time for a break up. It's time to trade up. There is Someone better for you. There is more for you.

CHAPTER 7

ENCOURAGEMENT INSULATES AND IGNITES

"But encourage one another daily, as long as it is called 'Today,' so that none of you may be hardened by sin's deceitfulness."

HEBREWS 3:13

When I was young, my Dad said, "Matt, you may never know how just one smile could change someone's whole day." Since it wasn't humanly possible to encourage or share Jesus with everyone he saw in passing, my Dad made a point to extend kindness whenever possible, even by simply smiling.

Encouragement has the power to alter the course not only of someone's day but also their life. There are at least two main ways in which encouragement impacts our lives.

GET INSULATED FROM SIN

First, encouragement insulates us from the tendency to sin. It helps keep our hearts soft toward God and His ways. That's what God said in Hebrews 3:13 (NIV).

> "But encourage one another daily, as long as it is called 'Today,' so that none of you may be hardened by sin's deceitfulness."

To encourage someone is to steer them toward God and away from sin—that's powerful. Godly encouragement softens us to God. On the other hand, when we lack encouragement, we are more prone to become hardened to Him. And when we become hardened against God, we distance ourselves from Him. In doing so, we expose ourselves to attack and defeat by the enemy. An unencouraged heart is an unbelief-prone heart. A downcast heart is wide open to demonic deception. In contrast, the person who has an encouraged heart will be shielded from satanic enticements.

As a culture, we underestimate and understate the potency of encouragement. According to Hebrews 3:13 (see above), how often do we need encouragement? Every day, no exceptions. *God* says to encourage one another daily. But in reality, how often do other people encourage you? How often do you encourage those you know? Probably not daily.

Maybe you are like me in that I sometimes lose sight of the most basic and essential spiritual principles (including the need to uplift the downcast). We are fickle and forgetful people. What was top-of-mind one minute quickly gets shuffled to the background. But I don't forget because of memory loss or because "the basics" are too complex to comprehend. No, my mind forgets because my heart forgets. Life can sometimes be a rollercoaster. I may feel up today, then down tomorrow. I see what is around me. I see who is around me, and I may become discouraged. I read some bad news. As a result of our surroundings and circumstances, we can subconsciously allow our emotions to dictate how we think, talk, and live.

Godly encouragement has received far too little press in our generation. Instead of looking for ways to encourage the good in others, we live in a culture that searches out and even fabricates human faults. Instead of practicing building others up, it has become customary to tear them down. Instead of supernaturally mending the broken, it has become second nature to rip others for their failures.

GET IGNITED FOR GOD

When we receive encouragement, we are not only insulated from the tendency to sin but also ignited to walk closer with God. Think of encouragement as gas on God's fire in our hearts. Again, I'm not talking about fluffy flattery. Not at all. Neither am I advocating that we ignore what Paul wrote to the Galatians (6:1 NIV) when he said,

> "Brothers and sisters, if someone is caught in a sin, you

who live by the Spirit should restore that person gently. But watch yourselves, or you also may be tempted."

Sometimes encouragement means sharing something hard to hear with someone who has gone off track.[18] But it is to always be in a spirit of gentleness to restore and redirect them back to the Lord.

Servant encouragers are very rare. That is not to shame anyone, but that's just the reality. The same was true when Paul lived. When writing to the Philippians, Paul said of Timothy, "For I have no one like him, who will be genuinely concerned for your welfare" (Phil. 2:20).

If the Bible says we should encourage one another daily, then the implication is that we all need daily encouragement. Simply because someone may *appear* to be doing fine doesn't mean they are. As a result, it's easy to live oblivious to the discouraged souls hiding in plain sight all around us.

But since encouragement is so rare, do you know what that means? When you are the encourager and reach out to encourage someone, it matters more than you may ever know. Everyone is going through something. You could be the only voice or face of encouragement someone receives that day, month, year, or even during their lifetime. I'm astonished to learn that I'm often the first, or maybe second, person to invest the time to really get to know someone (e.g., by simply listening, by buying them a meal, etc.).

Encouragement Insulates and Ignites

If you sense the Holy Spirit urging you to encourage someone, do it. How you love someone—what you share with or do for them—could be remembered for a lifetime. It might forever change her life, his life. What you speak could dislodge lies that have festered in someone's mind for years. What you say or do could be powerfully used "for building up" another person in ways you may never realize. As Paul instructs us,

> "What then, brothers? When you come together, each one has a hymn, a lesson, a revelation, a tongue, or an interpretation. *Let all things be done for building up*" (1 Cor. 14:26).

I now want to share a couple of real-life examples that reveal the life-altering impact of biblical encouragement.

Joshua is the first case study. In Joshua 1:9, Joshua was encouraged by the Lord when the time came to begin the conquest of the Promised Land: "Have I not commanded you? Be strong and courageous. Do not be afraid; do not be discouraged, for the LORD your God will be with you wherever you go." God encouraged Joshua when he was afraid and needed courage the most.

Discouragement stalls us from advancing God's Kingdom. Joshua needed great courage to do what God had asked of him.

But rewind to an event recorded in Numbers 13. I want to highlight a detail that often gets overlooked in the story of

The Twelve Spies. I believe that Joshua may not have done what he did—or been who he was—without the encouragement of a specific someone years earlier. That someone was Caleb. When everyone else faltered in fear, Caleb alone stood firm in faith. Not even Moses initially joined him.

Nevertheless, we always hear about Moses and also Joshua, who later courageously led the people against the demonic giants of Canaan. But we rarely hear about Caleb, who first "led" Joshua by his daring example of courage. Caleb, not Joshua, "quieted the people before Moses and said, 'Let us go up at once and occupy it, the land, for we are well able to overcome it'" (Num. 13:30). Joshua did not stand up, not initially anyway. Caleb did. In the chapters following Numbers 13, we learn that Caleb's example prompted Joshua also to be courageous. The Lord chose Joshua to lead the people into that Promised Land, but Caleb was instrumental in his development as that leader. Joshua would not have been who he was if there was no Caleb. Never underestimate how your courage might *en*courage others.

Likewise, Paul would not be who he was without the encouragement of another individual. As a new convert, Luke wrote this about Paul in Acts 9:26: "And when he had come to Jerusalem, he attempted to join the disciples. And they were all afraid of him, for they did not believe that he was a disciple." The other believers looked at Paul and may have said something to themselves like, "This guy just got finished spilling the blood of our friends and family. He hates us, and we don't buy it. We see him preaching, but we don't believe he's a genuine follower of Jesus." Then something changed. Read on in verses 27-30:

> "*But Barnabas took him and brought him to the apostles* and declared to them how on the road he had seen the Lord, who spoke to him, and how at Damascus he had preached boldly in the name of Jesus. So he went in and out among them at Jerusalem, preaching boldly in the name of the Lord. And he spoke and disputed against the Hellenists. But they were seeking to kill him. *And when the brothers learned this, they brought him down to Caesarea and sent him off to Tarsus.*"

Paul was initially rejected by many in the Church. But one man, Barnabas, stepped in at the risk of his own reputation and said (paraphrased), "Hey, you know what? I will believe that Paul is who he says he is and encourage what God is already clearly doing in and through him." How much did Barnabas' encouragement matter? A lot! It had a significant ripple effect. Notice verse 31 (of Acts 9): "So the church throughout all Judea and Galilee and Samaria had peace and was being built up. And walking in the fear of the Lord and in the comfort of the Holy Spirit, it multiplied."

Paul's ministry continued because of one person's encouragement, and the Church was built-up (or encouraged) and multiplied. One man's encouragement affected Paul, but that was just in the short term. Later in Acts 20:1-2, Paul traveled to multiple cities to encourage the believers. Wow, the perpetual multiplication effect of encouragement.

Paul not only realized the emphasis God puts on encouragement but also experienced its profound effects in his own life. Even though frequently overlooked in our modern Christian culture, Paul repeatedly wrote about the importance of encouragement.

For example, he reminded the Thessalonians to continue to "encourage the fainthearted" and "encourage one another and build one another up, just as you are doing" (see 1 Thess. 5:14, 11). He sent Tychicus to the Ephesian and the Colossian Churches for one purpose on at least two occasions. Why? You guessed it; it was to encourage them. He repeated the exact words verbatim to both groups of believers when he wrote, "I have sent him to you for this very purpose, that you may know how we are, and that he may encourage your hearts" (see Eph. 6:22 and Col. 4:8). Paul realized the importance and lasting effect of encouragement. His resolve to encourage others lived on as long as he had breath.

CHAPTER 8

ENCOURAGEMENT BREEDS ENCOURAGERS

"Blessed be the God and Father of our Lord Jesus Christ, the Father of mercies and God of all comfort, who comforts us in all our affliction, so that we may be able to comfort those who are in any affliction, with the comfort with which we ourselves are comforted by God."

2 CORINTHIANS 1:3-4

His life was drawing to a close. With the end in sight, Paul found himself in the most undesirable and unexpected retirement. He spent the final days of his life on lockdown in Rome. He was wrongfully confined to his home on house arrest for about two years. How did Paul react to that situation? What was his m.o. (modus operandi) during that time? How did he spend his final days?

THE ENCOURAGED BECOMES THE ENCOURAGER

Among other things, Paul wrote a letter to the Philippian believers to encourage them. While on house arrest in Rome around AD 60[19], Paul could have complained about his horrible circumstances. But instead, he wrote a letter about joy. What?! While mistreated, Paul shared words of encouragement that have endured far beyond his life and temporary trials. Instead of dwelling on what should have disappointed him, he considered the well-being of those who lived thousands of miles away.

Even though he was in far greater need of encouragement than they were, Paul crafted a letter to encourage his friends. He looked away from his needs to the needs of others. Longing to be with them, he prayed for them with joy in his heart and encouragement in his words.

Like Paul, how can you and I bring great encouragement to others even when our discouragement is great? What was Paul's secret to acting opposite to his circumstances? How was it possible that the one in the most need of encouragement actually gave the most encouragement to others? What Paul did seems backward. The one who was restricted shared about freedom. Even when embattled, Paul encouraged others to fight. Void of circumstantial enjoyment, he shared joy with others. Such behavior should have been impossible, except for one thing. To what "one thing" am I referring? The one thing that changed everything for Paul was none other than the one Person who can change anything for anyone. Paul looked past what he saw to Him who saw him. Paul was "looking to Jesus, the founder and perfecter of our faith, who for the joy that was set before him endured the cross" (Heb. 12:2a). Like Jesus told Martha, "one thing is necessary," which is to sit "at the Lord's feet" (see Luke 10:38-42).

When Paul wrote to the Philippians, he rhetorically said this in chapter two, verse one: "So if there is any encouragement in Christ…" (see Phil. 2:1). Is there any encouragement in Christ? Yes! The only way Paul could encourage others was because he met with Encouragement Himself. Encouragement has a name; His name is Jesus. Even if it flows through someone else, God Himself is upstream from all godly encouragement. Our encouragement to encourage others is ultimately found in Jesus. Paul knew that.

It might seem obvious, but we cannot be continually encouraged by Jesus unless we first frequently come to Him. We can only encourage others once we have first let Jesus encourage us. Nothing less than being enamored with God's grace for us will enable us to impart that same grace to others. Paul said, "But by the grace of God I am what I am, and his grace toward me was not in vain. On the contrary, I worked harder than any of them, *though it was not I, but the grace of God that is with me*" (1 Cor. 15:10). Paul's words were consistent with what Jesus said in John 15:4—"Abide in me, and I in you. As the branch cannot bear fruit by itself, unless it abides in the vine, neither can you, unless you abide in me."

In Jesus, Paul had the best possible example of what to do during difficulty. So do we. Let me put it this way. Who cared for Jesus when He was in the most pain of His life on the Cross? Who looked out for His needs? Who encouraged Him? No one. Yet Jesus encouraged others even while experiencing extreme suffering.

Nearing death on the Cross, "when Jesus saw his mother and the disciple whom he loved standing nearby, he said to his mother, 'Woman, behold, your son!' Then he said to the disciple, 'Behold, your mother!' And from that hour the disciple took her to his own home" (John 19:26-27). He cared for His mother even when no one cared for Him. Jesus looked to the needs of others even when others looked away from Him.

When we come to Jesus, He imparts His courage to us. He encourages us. He gives us His ability to encourage others. But the courage He gifts to us is intended to be regifted.

With intense love in his heart, Paul wrote this to the Church in Rome:

> "For I long to see you, that I may *impart* to you some spiritual gift to *strengthen you*—that is, that *we may be*

mutually encouraged by each other's faith, both yours and mine" (Rom. 1:11-12).

THE BEST ENCOURAGERS HAVE BEEN THE MOST DISCOURAGED

Because our God is committed to encouraging and comforting us (directly and indirectly through others), we also have the privilege of doing the same. Paul affirmed that truth in his second letter to the Corinthian Church (1:3-4), saying,

> "Blessed be the God and Father of our Lord Jesus Christ, the Father of mercies and God of *all comfort*, who comforts us in all our affliction, *so that we may be able to comfort those who are in any affliction*, with the comfort with which we ourselves are comforted by God."

Ironically, those who have been the most discouraged are often the best equipped to comfort or encourage others. When you feel the least competent to give is when you can and should give the most. Even when you have nothing, your Father has everything… and He loves to share!

Even when a demonic "messenger of Satan" whispers, or even yells, words in your ear "to harass" you (see 2 Cor. 12:7), you should declare like Paul did that "when I am weak, then I am strong" (2 Cor. 12:10b). No messenger will ever overpower the powerful message of the gospel, which is embodied in Jesus Himself.

Even though you may sometimes feel dry, "as the Scripture said, 'From his innermost being will flow rivers of living water'" (John 7:38b NASB). Neither drought in your soul nor lack in your life can limit what the Almighty can do in and through a willing vessel.

When in your discouragement you encourage someone else, the strangest thing happens. A mysterious, divine dichotomy transpires. The encourager becomes the encouraged. What may feel backward to give will come back to you. When you pour out even in your lack, it will come back. Proverbs 11:25 says, "Whoever brings blessing will be enriched, and one who waters will himself be watered."

When you speak blessing over someone, you impart God's grace and encouragement to them (see Num. 6:22-27; Eph. 4:29). When you encourage others even when you are low, you will lift them because they will see the great Encourager shining in your face. And when that occurs, the most remarkable thing will have happened. Like John the Baptist, you will have pointed someone to Jesus. As Jesus said in Luke 7:28, "I tell you, among those born of women none is greater than John. Yet the one who is least in the kingdom of God is greater than he."

If you are discouraged, encouraging others is the most challenging and unnatural thing to do. That is why, in your "leastness," you must draw near Jesus to draw on His endlessness.

The antidote for discouragement is to first come to Encouragement Himself, to Jesus. And as quickly as you have become "the encouraged," then go as "the encourager." First, come, then go. You can't give what you don't have, what you haven't yet received. And the only place to get what you don't have but need most is from Jesus. First seek Him, then seek out someone else. When discouragement fills your heart, it's time for encouragement to fill your mouth. Practically speaking, when the demonic darts of discouragement are launched at you, you can lift the shield of faith by uplifting someone else. Allow me to elaborate. The imperative of Ephesians 6:16 is to "In all circumstances *take up* the shield of faith, with which you can extinguish *all* the flaming darts of the evil one."

Before we can take up the shield of faith, we must first know what in the world that even means. Well, what is faith? I know what it is not: faith is not a belief. It is an action. If you have doubts about the veracity of that statement, then contrast the *actions* of the faith heroes of Hebrews 11 with what James said: "Even the demons believe—and shudder" (James 2:19b)! No wonder Paul used the action words "take up" to describe what we should do with this shield. And it is no coincidence that just two verses following that directive he told the Ephesians to "be persistent in your prayers for all believers everywhere" (see Eph. 6:18b NLT). God is essentially conveying that, against the enemy, the best defense is a good offense.

If Paul encouraged others with pen and parchment under house arrest, we can do the same in person, with our smartphones, on a video call, via prayer, by publishing a blog or book—or however God directs. We have enormously more at our fingertips to encourage one another than Paul did. Yet even with more, we often encourage less.

Maybe God is speaking to you even now; maybe there's someone He is urging you to uplift. Go and encourage them. Or at least pray for them. And don't expect a discouraged person to seek you out for encouragement. They probably won't. It's on you to discern their need. We have grown accustomed to holding our cards close to our chest in our society. We have learned how to hide when we need help. Let's try something different. Let's proactively pray for others, especially when we sense that they may need extra prayer. Let's reach out to others, not even waiting for an invitation. Like Jesus, let's simply love expecting nothing in return (see Matt. 5:43-48). If the Spirit impresses you to pray something or say something, pray it or say it! But also be ready if someone does approach you for help.

On a particular occasion, some family friends reached out to us asking for prayer for one of their children. They were discouraged. After promising to pray, I then asked them to also pray for one of our children, who was also having a tough week.

The very next morning, a wonderful thing happened. We received an encouraging text from our friends, assuring us that they had been praying for us. We were encouraged by the same people who had reached out for encouragement just one day earlier. The ones who were previously discouraged became encouraged encouragers.

Every time someone reaches out to me for encouragement, it is always my joy to encourage them. But I don't stop there; I often try to take it a step further. I'm vulnerable with them as they've been to me. For their sake, I invite them to also offer their help to me in some way because I know that they will be most blessed themselves when they bless others. I "remember the words of the Lord Jesus, how he himself said, 'It is more blessed to give than to receive'" (Acts 20:35b).

When you *en*courage, you implant courage into the heart of another warrior. When you give encouragement, you give hope at just the time when it's needed most.

It's time to take courage from above so that you can lift up those buried beneath demonic mountains of *dis*couragement.

PART 3

COUNTERING THE ENEMY

It's time to defeat what defeats you

CHAPTER 9

COME BURDENED

"Come to me, all who labor and are heavy laden, and I will give you rest."

MATTHEW 11:28

Are you perpetually nagged by a general sense of guilt or condemnation? If so, when you feel that way, you probably aren't too inclined to cry out to God for help. Listen to the following story Jesus shared in Luke 18:9-14 (NLT).

> "Then Jesus told this story to some who had great confidence in their own righteousness and scorned everyone else: ''Two men went to the Temple to pray. One was a Pharisee, and the other was a despised tax collector. The Pharisee stood by himself and prayed this prayer: 'I thank you, God, that I am not a sinner like everyone else. For I don't cheat, I don't sin, and I don't commit adultery. I'm certainly not like that tax collector! I

fast twice a week, and I give you a tenth of my income.' But the tax collector stood at a distance and dared not even lift his eyes to heaven as he prayed. Instead, he beat his chest in sorrow, saying, 'O God, be merciful to me, for I am a sinner.' I tell you, this sinner, not the Pharisee, returned home justified before God. For those who exalt themselves will be humbled, and those who humble themselves will be exalted.'"

Which character from this story best describes you? The Pharisee or the tax collector? Do you often fixate on others' failures, or do you recognize your need for God's help? Determining whose sandals you best fit into will help you sort out the *true* condition of your heart.

Do you regularly seek Jesus, or are you reluctant to spend time with Him? If the second is true, have you ever wondered why? Like the Pharisee, anyone who doesn't realize their need for Jesus will *not* seek Him. Alternatively, as Jesus's story reveals, the person who asks for forgiveness *will* receive it. If you are that person, you are far better off than you may realize… because Jesus declares you are now "justified!"

Paul opened *all* of his letters to the churches by greeting his fellow Christians as "saints" (or sometimes just "the church(es)").[20] But he *never* addressed them as "sinners." You have a new title in Christ. God calls you a saint (literally meaning "most holy thing"[21]). Even though we all sin and still need to repent, "sinner" is attached to our former identity. Because of Jesus, you have "become the righteousness of God" (see 2 Cor. 5:21).

I've known many Christians who feel so bad about feeling bad that they remain stuck in a rut of "re-repenting" for sins from which the Father has already forgiven them. If you *feel* God's default disposition toward you is condemnation, someone has been lying to you. "Even if we feel guilty, God is greater than our feelings, and he knows everything" (1 John 3:20 NLT). In his gospel account (3:17-18), John was emphatic that,

> "For God did *not* send His Son into the world to condemn the world, but that the world through Him might be saved. He who believes in Him is not condemned; but he who does not believe is condemned already, because he has not believed in the name of the only begotten Son of God."

Once you are reborn into God's family by faith in Jesus (see John 1:11-13), once you are "in Christ Jesus," you are no longer condemned, no longer guilty in the courtroom of Heaven. Instead, God pronounces you as innocent because "Therefore there is now *no* condemnation *at all* for those who are in Christ Jesus" (Rom. 8:1 NASB).

Do you know Jesus intimately? If so, then you have eternal life. Jesus said, "And this is eternal life, that they *know* you, the only true God, and Jesus Christ whom you have sent"

(John 17:3). Knowing Jesus is *not* to be confused with knowing *about* Jesus. Do you know Jesus to a deeper degree than even that of your closest human relation (e.g., your spouse)? That's the level of knowing that Jesus intended to convey in John 17:3.[22]

DON'T BE SHAMED INTO NOT COMING

But even if you know Jesus and have "become the righteousness of God in Him" (2 Cor. 5:21b NKJV), the evil one, the accuser, still yells out "day and night" (see Rev. 12:10) that you will never be good enough to come to God. As true as that once was without Jesus (see Rom. 3:10, 23), Jesus is good enough to approach the Father on your behalf (see 1 Tim. 2:5). He came for you so you could come to the Father. Jesus said, "I did not come to call the righteous, but sinners" (Mark 2:17b NASB).

The disgraced and defeated devil (see Col. 2:15) may claim that you are too shamefully broken and spent to seek God's help. But Isaiah (42:3a) prophesied about Jesus that "a bruised reed he will not break, and a faintly burning wick he will not quench."

The father of lies (see John 8:44) may whisper that God doesn't want you, so you might as well not come. But in John 14:18a (NIV), Jesus promised that He "will not leave you as orphans."

The same devil who convinces many religious leaders to "load people with burdens hard to bear" (see Luke 11:46) tells you that you are too burdened and burned out to come. But Jesus extends this invite in Matthew 11:28: "Come to me, all who labor and are heavy laden, and I will give you rest."

"The dragon and his angels" (see Rev. 12:7) breathe out a caustic narrative to convince you that God has shunned you because you can never be "spiritual" enough. On the contrary, Jesus welcomes the weak, distressed, and humble—He said, "Blessed are the poor in spirit, for theirs is the kingdom of heaven. Blessed are those who mourn, for they shall be comforted. Blessed are the meek, for they shall inherit the earth" (Matt. 5:3-5).

The accuser is a sin sniffer, but Jesus is a sin squelcher. In Hebrews 8:12 (NIV), God declares, "For I will forgive their wickedness and will remember their sins no more."

Satan will try to intimidate you. But even though his bark is loud, God has taken away his bite. "He disarmed the rulers and authorities and put them to open shame, by triumphing over them in him" (Col. 2:15). In the fifth chapter (verse 8) of his first epistle, Peter exposed the devil as roaming around "like" a roaring lion. In my wife's words, "The devil is a poser, an impersonator, there is only one true Lion: 'the Lion of the tribe of Judah'! Satan wants us to think he is a lion, but he is only one to those whom he has convinced. His authority is as good as his acting skills." Well said!

Don't listen to anything spoken by "the prince of the power of the air" (see Eph. 2:2) because he is full of hot air. Satan, "that serpent of old" (see Rev. 12:9 NKJV), is the original and biggest sinner of all (see 1 John 3:8). Yet, he hypocritically accuses us of the same sins he tempts us to think, say or do in the first place. Don't entertain what he thinks of you and tells you, even for a minute. He is doomed (see Rev. 20:10). But if you know and love Jesus, hear this: "For I know the thoughts that I think toward you, says the LORD, thoughts of peace and not of evil, to give you a future and a hope" (Jer. 29:11 NKJV).

DON'T BE SLOW TO COME

Indeed, the best time to run to Jesus is when you feel the worst, when life is at its worst. In Matthew 11:28, Jesus said, "Come to me, *all who labor and are heavy laden*, and I will give you rest." Jesus extends an invitation. Whether or not you already personally know Jesus, this invitation is for *you*. No matter what you carry, you qualify to come to Jesus.

Regardless of what condition you're in, what matters is that you simply come. Jesus extends His invitation to *all* who "labor and are heavy laden." If He said that "all" are *invited* to come, guess what that means? All *need* to come, no exceptions or exclusions. No matter what you have done, the Truth will always stand "For *by grace* you have been saved through faith. And this is *not* your own doing; it is the gift of God, *not a result of works*, so that no one may boast" (Eph. 2:8-9). "If we confess our sins, he is faithful and just and *will* forgive us our sins and purify us from all unrighteousness" (1 John 1:9 NIV).

In those moments when life gets hard, we have a choice. We can either turn to Jesus or away from Him. What is the pattern of your life? When things feel out of control, where do you go? Either way, He is willing and able to help you *right now*. We all carry burdens that we were *not* built to bear. They are too heavy for me, too heavy for you, *but* not for Jesus. It is His joy to free us from what has had us caged.

There can sometimes be a sense that what I'm going through will just go away or wear off on its own. Just give it enough time, right? Does time heal all wounds? No. But God can. By putting off coming to God, I am putting my hope in the false "god" of time. God often uses time to help heal our hearts, but time, in and of itself, isn't the answer. Jesus is. The very instant you are under the attack of the enemy, your best option is *always* to run beneath the protective wings of the Almighty (see Ps. 91:1-7). I've lost count of how many times I've met with Jesus throughout my life and been changed simply by being with Him.

Waiting for change without waiting on the Change-Maker is a waste of time. "The Lord is good to those who wait *for him*, to the soul who seeks him" (Lam. 3:25). To "wait" is the Hebrew word qāvâ, which can also be translated as "look for, hope, expect."[23] We find God's blessing when we hope in, expect, or wait "for *him*." It does *not* say, "God is good to those who do nothing or hope in themselves." We don't get extra points for going it alone.

For many years after having braces as an adolescent, I wore a retainer bar in my mouth to keep my teeth aligned. But many years later, as an adult, that retainer broke. The longer I waited to go to the orthodontist—the only person who could fix the problem—the more my teeth got out of whack. My once completely straight teeth got so bad that I needed to pay several thousand dollars for uncomfortable braces. All over again.

Not only did waiting not fix the issue, but it got worse. When something is broken, time actually works against us. The longer we delay addressing a problem, the worse it gets. Whereas dealing with it right away can alleviate many unnecessary problems and pain.

We need to continually come to Jesus so that He can keep us "aligned" with Him. Just like my teeth, we always have forces pulling on us. But without Jesus as the more potent counterforce, we will find ourselves more aligned with the world around us. Rather than changing the world for the better, it will change us for the worse.

The "flaming darts of the evil one" (Eph. 6:1b) and the "fiery trials" of life (see 1 Pet. 4:12 NLT) do not just magically roll off of our backs like water. We aren't ducks. Battles and burdens are often like barnacles. My father-in-law, who served in the U.S. Navy, once shared with me about the necessity of periodically removing the barnacles from the ship on which he was stationed. If the sailors neglected to remove those sticky crustaceans, the boat would eventually lose its ability to cut through the water.

In the same way, when we come to the Lord, He helps us get free of the "barnacles" we've picked up along the way on the sea of life. It is difficult to put words to how it happens. It just does. But even though the Spirit's miraculous work in us is inexpressible, it doesn't make it any less life-changing. When we bring our burdens to Jesus, He takes them.

According to 1 John 5:18, even in the battles, Jesus "protects" "everyone who has been born of God" "and the evil one does not touch him." When I give Jesus my burdens, I get Him and His help to fight my battles. Every time I sit with "my shepherd," "He restores my soul" (see Ps. 23:1, 3a). I walk to Him weak, with arms drooping and head down, but always leave with "new strength" given by "the lifter of my head" (see Isa. 40:31 NLT; Ps. 3:3b).

But usually, when we are in the most need, we are the least likely to ask for help. But Hebrews 4:14-16 (NKJV) flies in the face of that norm. It says,

> "Seeing then that we have a great High Priest who has passed through the heavens, Jesus the Son of God, let us hold fast our confession. For we do not have a High Priest who cannot sympathize with our weaknesses, but was in all points tempted as we are, yet without sin. Let us therefore come boldly to the throne of grace,

that we may obtain mercy and find grace to help *in time of need*."

When are we supposed to come to find grace and mercy? What does it say? Verse 16: "In time of need"! Not only when you feel good. No, Jesus says to come to Him even in the middle of your mess or while poor in spirit.

DON'T "BE STRONG" OR YOU WON'T COME

Never let your great need keep you from your great God. Need is like appetite. The hungrier you are, the more you'll eat. So also, the more in need you are, the more desperate you will be for the Father's help. The greater your need, the louder your cry for help. The weaker you realize you are, the more likely you are to seek God's strength—and, in turn, the stronger you will become. It is in weakness that we are stretched to the point of dependence. Weakness is a blessing in disguise because God gift-wraps His strength in our weakness. Weakness, as the Bible uses it, refers to human frailty. Jesus was weak; He was "beset with weakness" and was "yet without sin" (see Heb. 5:2; 4:15). It's okay to admit that you're weak. Jesus experienced great weakness but also exuded great power. Weakness is *not* sin but unwillingness to acknowledge we are weak is—that's called pride. Anyone who holds on to pride will not and can not hold on to God.

So if human frailty, in and of itself, is *not* wrong, then why do so many Christians try to hide their weaknesses? If Paul, arguably the most prominent early Church leader, boasted "all the more gladly" of his "weaknesses, so that the power of Christ may rest upon" him (see 2 Cor. 12:9), then why do many modern-day Church leaders default to a "tough guy" / "tough gal" act? I believe that Satan has convinced much of the Church that weakness is the same as sin and shame. The devil has, in turn, played off of people's pride to stifle the display of God's power on earth. "But we have this treasure in jars of clay, to show that the surpassing power belongs to God and not to us" (2 Cor. 4:7). As an act of faith, agree with God by vocalizing this: "Let *the weak say*, 'I am strong'" (Joel 3:10b NKJV). God's "power is made perfect in weakness" (see 2 Cor. 12:9).

The self-reliant facade of "I'm good, I don't need anyone" may be the way of the world, but it's not the way of the Kingdom, of the King. Thankfully, our kind King can relate to our need to draw on the strength of the Father because that's what He did continually—"In the days of his flesh, Jesus offered up prayers and supplications, with loud cries and tears" (Heb. 5:7a). Jesus knows exactly what you're going through. He gets you. No one understands you like Him—*no one*. He created you, but He also knows what it's like to be human. The truth is, He wants to be near you *all* the time. It's time to offer all of you to Him. Weakness is nothing to wallow in or be ashamed of. Human deficiency should instead be a catalyst to come as a child to your all-strong Father and ever-sympathetic Savior.

CHAPTER 10

COME HELPLESS

"At that time Jesus declared, 'I thank you, Father, Lord of heaven and earth, that you have hidden these things from the wise and understanding and revealed them to little children.'"

MATTHEW 11:25

I sat alone in the cold night. Stillness filled the air. The moon blanketed the meadows with its soft glow. But despite my tranquil surroundings, a flurry of feelings seemed to silence the quietness. Pressing through a bog of distracting thoughts, I opened my mouth: "Father, I'm here as long as it takes." I continued, "I'm here to be with You. I have cleared my schedule for You. I want to hear Your heart and listen to Your voice. I don't know what to do. I need You." I waited. Nothing.

As I peered into the dark distance, I felt demonic darts of doubt begin to penetrate my mind. A thought entered my mind: "Will I actually get the help I need?" But even though

I felt nothing, in faith, I proceeded to seek God all the more. I had determined not to give up until I got what I had come for. I persisted in God's presence for the next few hours until I sensed an unseen shift.

I first learned how to whole-heartedly seek Jesus when I was a young adult (many years ago). I would regularly drive out into the quiet countryside, park my car, and spend time alone with my best Friend. I would pray, read, sing, and engage with my Father. I lingered there *until* my heart became lighter. Sometimes, what I sought took 20 minutes to find. Other times, I wrestled for two hours or more. But no matter how much time it took, each time I came poor, I always left rich. Each time I came empty, I always left overflowing. Each time I came dry, I always left refreshed. Each time I came hungry, I always left satisfied.

Even though seeking Jesus looks different for me nowadays, I still constantly pursue Him. After all these years, my perspective has remained unchanged: I still see myself as God's child and He as my Father. I still seek His guidance daily. I still need His help as much as ever. He is my life, my everything.

No more can we expect a child to solve the world's woes than are you and I expected to go it alone apart from God. Good for us that our Father is also God of the universe. More than that, Jesus "*always* lives to make intercession for them" who are His (see Heb. 7:25 NKJV). The best way to help ourselves is *not* to try to help ourselves. I realize that might sound contradictory or even nonsensical. But the best thing we can do when we need help is to get help. Put another way; God *doesn't* expect you to help yourself before coming to Him for help.

TRUST LIKE A LITTLE KID

But even though everyone needs God's help, why don't more seek it? Because not everyone is aware of or will admit their need. Spiritual malnourishment is everyone's default condition, but surprisingly many are unwilling to come to humankind's only source of life: Jesus. That's the catch: *each of us* must come to Jesus. Doing nothing won't change anything. But nothing moves Jesus's heart like the desperate cry of those who realize they are helpless. We can run to Him today with the same heart attitude we originally had. It was "for while we were still helpless, at the right time Christ died for the ungodly" (Rom. 5:6 NASB).

God's banquet table is only open to "little children." Directly *before* Jesus's well-known Matthew 11:28 invitation to "Come to me, all who labor and are heavy laden, and I will give you rest," He laid out the prerequisite to coming: having a childlike heart. Since only children recognize the necessity of depending on their father, it is children to whom Jesus reveals the Father. Jesus said the following to the Pharisees who refused to humble themselves, who couldn't seem to get past their own egos and intellect. Read verses 21-27 of Matthew 11.

> "'Woe to you, Chorazin! Woe to you, Bethsaida! *For if the mighty works done in you had been done in Tyre and Sidon, they would have repented long ago* in sackcloth and ashes. But I tell you, it will be more bearable on the day of judgment for Tyre and Sidon than for you. And you, Capernaum, will you be exalted to heaven? You will be brought down to Hades. *For if the mighty works done in you had been done in Sodom, it would have remained until this day.* But I tell you that it will be more tolerable on the day of judgment for the land of Sodom than for you.' At that time Jesus declared, 'I thank you, Father, Lord of heaven and earth, that you have hidden these things from the wise and understanding and revealed them to little children; yes, Father, for such was your gracious will. All things have been handed over to me by my Father, and no one knows the Son except the Father, and no one knows the Father except the Son and anyone to whom the Son chooses to reveal him.'"

Instead of resulting in turning the heavy-*hearted to* Jesus, "mighty works" often repel the heavy-*headed away from* Him. What is too hard for the mind to understand often hardens the heart. Because they couldn't comprehend miraculous works, the Pharisees and their followers rejected the cardinal miracle worker.

In the Matthew 11 passage above, Jesus repeated the exact phrase twice: "For if the mighty works done in you had been done in..." In both instances, what did Jesus state is the intended outcome of mighty works? They are meant to prompt belief and repentance. Wooing people with the Father's love to faith in Jesus has always been the purpose of performing mighty miraculous deeds (see Matt. 9:35-36). Here is what John wrote about the end goal of "miraculous signs:"

> "The disciples saw Jesus do many other miraculous signs in addition to the ones recorded in this book. *But these are written so that you may continue to believe* that Jesus is the Messiah, the Son of God, and that by believing in him you will have life by the power of his name" (John 20:30-31 NLT).

That said, even Jesus's disciples sometimes had difficulty accepting what they saw and heard modeled by their Master. In John 14:10-11, Jesus told Philip that if he wouldn't believe based on words alone, he should "at least believe on the evidence of the works themselves" (John 14:11b NIV).

Jesus's disciples eventually learned to trust their Master even when they didn't completely grasp what He said or did. But contrastingly, despite the Lord's best attempts, the Pharisees remained hard-hearted, just like their forefathers. As the Holy Spirit would later entreat through the writer of Hebrews (3:8-10),

> "Do not harden your hearts as in the rebellion, on the day of testing in the wilderness, where your fathers put me to

> the test and *saw my works for forty years.* Therefore I was provoked with that generation, and said, 'They always go astray in their heart; *they have not known my ways.*'"

God's signature way of working is supernaturally—it always has been. Moving through miracles *isn't* new for the Lord; they *aren't* New Testament only. Since "Jesus Christ is the same yesterday and today and forever" (Heb. 13:8), not a single aspect of God's character has ever changed, nor will it ever.

God *miraculously* protected and provided for the children of Israel. He parted the Red Sea and graciously gave food from the sky and water from rocks. Day and night, He supernaturally led the people through the desert in the form of a cloud and a pillar of fire. Miraculously, their sandals did not wear out. Yet, how God worked on their behalf often seemed strange to them. They were unthankful despite all He did for them. How deeply it must have hurt the Father's heart to be rejected by His creation. Because Israel thought nothing of God's miraculous works, they failed to understand His ways—while, in turn, disregarding His words.

Whenever anyone gets angry or tries to argue away God's miraculous wonders, you should wonder why. Rejecting the miraculous is precisely what the Pharisees exhibited throughout the gospel accounts and the book of Acts. Beyond what He said, none of Jesus's actions angered the Pharisees more than when He cast out demons, helped someone by healing them, or raised a dead person.

Instead of accepting Jesus's ways as a child, those religious scholars complicated what is simple enough for a child to understand. As the enemies of Christ, the Pharisees personified the opposite of the childlike faith required to enter the Kingdom of Heaven. "But Jesus said, 'Let the little children come to Me, and do not forbid them; for of such is the kingdom of heaven'" (Matt. 19:14 NKJV).

Consider a little child. My young son has never said, "Dad, you know what, I will pay the mortgage this month." Or, "I'm heading to the grocery store to buy food now (with the driver's license and credit card I don't have)." No, he doesn't do that. He, instead, simply and shamelessly tells me what he needs. Even though he doesn't completely understand *how* I provide for him, he doesn't worry that I will take care of him. My child just comes to me, 100% dependent when he needs something. We get to go to God with that same mindset and childlike heart. But more often than not, that's not easy to do. After all, we are adults, not children.

The author of Hebrews 11:6 (NKJV) wrote, "For he who comes to God must believe that He is, and that He is a rewarder of those who diligently seek Him." When you seek God, He will reward you with Himself (and some far less valuable extras like Jesus promised in Matthew 6:33). There is no greater reward than Jesus. He is the goal. Even when we may not see Him or feel Him, I pray that we remain committed to pursuing Jesus no matter what. The beginning of Proverbs 2 (verse 4) promises that you will find wisdom "if you seek it like silver and search for it as for hidden treasures"—and, according to Colossians 2:2-3 (NIV), Jesus is Wisdom personified:

> "My goal is that they may be encouraged in heart and united in love, so that they may have the full riches of complete understanding, in order that they may know the mystery of God, namely, *Christ, in whom are hidden all the treasures of wisdom and knowledge.*"

TUSSLE LIKE A BIG KID

Do you remember when Jacob persistently wrestled with God all night long? He was worried that his brother Esau would retaliate against him for the wrong Jacob had done against him years earlier. You can read that particular story in Genesis 32:22-32. Jacob essentially said to God (paraphrased), "I am not going to leave until *You* bless me" (see Gen. 32:26).

At first blush, demanding of God as Jacob did might seem self-centered. But let's look closer at the story. Why did Jacob so desperately seek the Lord's blessing? As you may recall, he had previously tried to get what he wanted through his own means: deceit and manipulation. He pragmatically acquired what he wanted (even God's blessing) by tricking others.

But with time, Jacob's approach to life and relationships changed. God was training Jacob to come to Him, his Father, for what he needed. Instead of "wrestling" with men, Jacob learned to take his worries, anger, fear, and desires all the way to the top, to God Himself. According to Genesis 32:24, he "wrestled" with God. That word ("'ābaq") can mean "grapple (get dusty)".[24]

If we are going to kick up dust, it is best to do it with God rather than with other men and women. It is commendable (and biblical) to wrestle with God in this sense.

Bringing your case directly to the Father stands in stark contrast with taking matters into our own hands. Jesus did the former by placing all of His trust in the Father. In so doing, He exemplified how much He trusted the Father. Of Jesus, Peter said,

> "When he was reviled, he did not revile in return; when he suffered, he did not threaten, but continued entrusting himself to him who judges justly" (1 Pet. 2:23).

Instead of taking your grievance to someone else, or worse, out on someone else, why not first take it to the top, to God Himself?! Why not come to "your Father [who] knows what you need before you ask him" (Matt. 6:8b)?[25] The Father invites us to come as Jacob came. But that was then. Even Jacob's example has been upgraded. In Hebrews 4:16 (NKJV), God instructs us to approach Him "boldly"!

> "Let us therefore come *boldly* to the throne of grace, that we may obtain mercy and find grace to help in time of need."

When you come to God for help, do not come sheepishly but boldly as one of His sheep. Your Father will not slap your hand when you bring your issues and needs to Him. He is, after all, the one who has told us to come. Those are His words to His beloved children. He is especially endeared to needy people. So go ahead and "wrestle" with your Father. Work through things with Him. Converse with Him. Be raw, be real.

Jacob knew God as Almighty, which He is. But thanks to Jesus, we now also know God as Aba (Papa or Daddy). How much more can and should we come boldly now?! We have full access to the Holiest of All as priests and as children of our Father. Jesus has ripped the veil wide open, welcoming us into our Dad's throne room, into His presence whenever and forever. We have full access to God, *but it is nevertheless up to us to come.*

In Luke 18:1-8 (NLT), the *Parable of the Persistent Widow*, Jesus shared a story to emphasize the need for persistent prayer.

> "One day Jesus told his disciples a story to show that they should always pray and never give up. 'There was a judge in a certain city,' he said, 'who neither feared God nor cared about people. A widow of that city came to him repeatedly, saying, 'Give me justice in this dispute with my enemy.' The judge ignored her for a while, but finally he said to himself, 'I don't fear God or care about people, but this woman is driving me crazy. I'm going to see that she gets justice, because she is wearing me out with her constant requests!'" Then the Lord said,

> 'Learn a lesson from this unjust judge. Even he rendered a just decision in the end. So don't you think God will surely give justice to his chosen people who cry out to him day and night? Will he keep putting them off? I tell you, he will grant justice to them quickly! But when the Son of Man returns, how many will he find on the earth who have faith?'"

Jesus said that it is in coming "repeatedly" to the Father with our "constant requests" and crying "out to him day and night" in prayer that we manifest faith on the earth (see Luke 18:3, 5, 8 NLT). As long as we ask with the right motives, we have God's permission to persist until we receive, seek until we find, and not give up until the door opens (see James 4:3; Luke 11:1-13).

Jesus's story is an invitation; it's an appeal to anyone who would listen about how much He wants us to ask of Him. He expects us to be expectant that He *will* answer our cries. If you sense Him calling you even now, I would advise you to set this book aside and spend some time seeking Him, waiting on Him.

He waits for *you*.

CHAPTER 11

COME INDIFFERENT

"And he said to them, 'Why are you sleeping? Rise and pray that you may not enter into temptation.'"

LUKE 22:46

A few years ago, I was asked a question during an interview to which most Christians can relate. The interviewer posed the question in the context of how my wife and I were willing to give up job security, income, and familiarity to transplant our family (on more than one occasion) simply because God asked us to do so. He put the question to me this way, "If I'm being honest with myself, I just don't care. I know I should care, but how do I get to that point, where my heart is so connected to Jesus that I see the value in people so much that I'm literally willing to give up 'everything'?"

ARE YOU NOT FEELIN' IT?

Even as a born-again believer, have you ever been disinterested in the things of God? Has your heart ever grown cold or complacent? (It's okay; you can be honest—it's just you and God.) You feel torn. You know you should care more but don't know what to do. You might assume the solution must be complicated. To fully follow Jesus will probably require more work or risk than you are willing to commit. Or worse, if you start caring, God will ask you to do something you don't want to do. You're not quite ready for that. "Maybe another day," you think to yourself. Avoiding the unknown by staying with what's familiar just seems easier. You push your conflicting thoughts to the background, yet again. As you shift your attention back to what has held you in a rut, you grow even more numb to the nagging reality that something is lacking.

Contrary to your thoughts, what you have been missing is not complicated. It's simple, singular. But more about that in the following chapter.

More often than not, our human default is to take the path of least resistance. To walk the road *more* traveled. To opt for what feels most convenient. Especially when faced with a difficult decision, I think it's safe to say that most people prefer to play it safe. Let's be honest; it's normal to gravitate to ease over difficulty. Can you relate? If that is you, you aren't alone. If you have ever felt those tendencies, then you are human.

Believe it or not, even Jesus experienced the same emotions. Hebrews 4:15 (NIV) affirms, "For we do not have a high priest who is unable to empathize with our weaknesses, but we have one who has been tempted in every way, just as we are—yet he did not sin."

JESUS WASN'T FEELIN' IT

As He approached the most agonizing and challenging experience ever endured (carrying all of humankind's sin to the Cross), Jesus said, "My soul is very sorrowful, even to death" (Matt. 26:38a). Before a single nail pierced His body, fiery arrows tore into His mind. Jesus was in the middle of an invisible battle. His internal struggle was so severe that He physically fell to the ground. Matthew recorded, "And going a little farther he fell on his face and prayed, saying, 'My Father, if it be possible, let this cup pass from me; nevertheless, not as I will, but as you will'" (Matt. 26:39). Jesus's internal war continued to rage. His resistance against the forces of evil grew so intense that it physically manifested again, but this time to an excruciating level. As Luke described it in his gospel account (22:44), "And being in agony he prayed more earnestly; and his sweat became like great drops of blood falling down to the ground." Even though you or I have "not yet *resisted* to the point of shedding your blood" (Heb. 12:4b NIV), Jesus did just that in the Garden of Gethsemane and later at the Cross.

Like you and me, Jesus was at a crossroads: get up and carry a cross or do what was easy. Jesus felt horrible. He fell down and even bled from His pores. But when knocked down, He didn't give up. When knocked down, not a single disciple came to His aid. Luke 22:45 says, "And when he rose from prayer, he came to the disciples and found them sleeping for *sorrow*." You may notice a similarity between Jesus and the disciples at this point: they both felt deep sorrow. However, Jesus's response to that sorrow completely differed from the disciples' reaction.

The disciples gave in to the temptation to give up. Yet Jesus pressed on. How was Jesus able to rise and continue while the others weren't? No, it was not just "because He was Jesus." How then? There was a "silver bullet" Jesus offered to His disciples—to *all* of His disciples: them and us, both then and now. There was one reason Jesus was able to press on even beyond the point of breaking. One reason. He sought strength from the only source of strength. Jesus found help at the feet of His Father. As recorded in Isaiah 50:7, with Jesus speaking in the first person during the time of His passion:

> "But the Lord GOD helps me; therefore I have not been disgraced; therefore I have set my face like a flint, and I know that I shall not be put to shame."

Earlier in the same chapter (50:4), Isaiah prophesied this about Jesus, again with Jesus speaking in the first person:

> "The Lord GOD has given me the tongue of those who are taught, that I may know how to sustain with a word him who is weary. Morning by morning he awakens; he awakens my ear to hear as those who are taught."

On that dark night in Gethsemane, Jesus shared a specific "word" with His weary disciples *before* they dozed off. He said, "Pray that you may not enter into temptation" (Luke 22:40b). Jesus then followed His own advice and prayed, pouring out His heart on bended knee and prostrate face (see Luke 22:41b; Matt. 26:39a). He spoke, then He modeled for us *the* example to follow. After waking the disciples (just four verses later), "He said to them, 'Why are you sleeping? Rise and pray that you may not enter into temptation'" (Luke 22:46).

What would have happened if the disciples had prayed and acted on Jesus's word? Jesus cleared up any ambiguity around that in Luke 22:40. When He said, "Pray that you may not enter into temptation," that's what He meant. In other words, *if* the disciples had prayed, they would *not* have fallen into temptation. Instead of sleeping, they would have stood strong alongside Jesus. That's what Jesus said would happen. Therefore, I know beyond a doubt that perseverance would have been those disciples' alternate reality in that instance. If they had prayed as prescribed, those shells of men would have sprung to life. They would have risen, filled with fresh hope. Prayer is a powerful antidote for anything that impedes our perseverance.

"Why are you sleeping? *Rise and pray that you may not enter into temptation*" (Luke 22:46). Jesus's words were, and still are, a promise. A promise, which He has given to you and me. He has handed us a silver bullet to "kill" the temptation to give up in the middle of the battle. "Praying at all times in the Spirit" (Eph. 6:18a) is pivotal for countering the tempter.

God's power will be available to us when we access His help through prayer and then act based on His promises. Even power enough "to sustain with a word him who is weary" (Isa. 50:4a). As Jesus put it, "The words that I have spoken to you are spirit and life" (John 6:63b). Whether in a garden or a desert, whether praying, or whether wielding Scripture and directly telling Satan to "be gone" (see Matt. 4:1-11), Jesus modeled how to resist the enemy and "in all circumstances take up the shield of faith" (Eph. 6:16a).

As Jesus exemplified, when we seek help from the Father, we will always find the strength to continue along His path for us. Do you know that Jesus's Father is also your Father? What is available to the Father's only begotten Son is now also available to those the Son calls His brothers and sisters. God states in Hebrews 2:11—"For he who sanctifies and those who are sanctified *all have one source*. That is why he is not ashamed to call them brothers."

As a man on earth, Jesus's source of strength was one and the same as our source. As the "one mediator between God and men" (see 1 Tim. 2:5), Jesus is the door through which we can access the same help He also received from the Father.

WHAT TO DO IF YOU'RE NOT FEELIN' IT

Fully aware of the full access we have to approach the Father, what can we glean from Jesus's prayer? Look at it again:

> "And going a little farther he fell on his face and prayed, saying, 'My Father, if it be possible, let this cup pass from me; nevertheless, not as I will, but as you will'" (Matt. 26:39).

Notice how raw that prayer was. From the very mouth of Jesus, we hear a confession of not wanting (want is another word for "will") to continue to the Cross. That may initially sound heretical, but it's not. It can be easy to overlook the honest humanity of His prayer. Like you and me, Jesus felt the human temptation to avoid anything hard or painful. But if we downplay any of Jesus's words on any justification, we reshape Him into our image—including reasoning like "Oh, Jesus couldn't have experienced this or that because He is God." Hebrews 4:15b (NIV) clearly states that, although the sinless Son of God, Jesus was "tempted in every way, just as we are." We must resist the urge to rework God's words or works to fit the limits of our cognitive comfort. To do so in this instance would be to rob God of an opportunity to "empathize with our weakness" (Heb. 4:15a NIV) as "a man of sorrows" (Isa. 53:3a).

In the honest prayer of our Lord, we find permission also to be honest. So *don't* let the realization that you may *not* want to yield to the "want" (or will) of the Father perpetuate feelings of condemnation. It's simply a reminder that you need help. A reminder that you cannot continue down God's path without God Himself.

If you don't want to do what you know you should do, simply ask Him to change your "want to." It really is that simple. No one wants to submit to someone else. Independence is our default want, but dependence on God is our greatest need. God always welcomes "I don't want to [fill in the blank]" prayers because they are admissions of our need for Him. To anyone slugging through the struggles of life, God says, "If any of you lacks wisdom, you should ask God, who gives generously to all *without finding fault*, and it *will* be given to you" (James 1:5 NIV).

When we are the most confused and the most overrun with hardship is precisely when God extends His helping hand. "Help" is actually an understatement. As the New King James Version declares, God wants to give us His wisdom "liberally" (see James 1:5 NKJV)!

When we seek His help, God *doesn't* embarrass us by reminding us of our failures or weaknesses. No, He embraces us as He empowers us. Our Father does not rub our noses in our downfalls. Instead, He is "the One who lifts my head high" (see Ps. 3:2-3 NIV). "Draw near to God, and he *will* draw near to you" (James 4:8a).

It's time to bring Jesus all your burdens, needs, and downheartedness, which often hide within.

It's time to view yourself through the eyes of your ever-loving Father, even if no one else does.

We cannot allow our past blunders or any tendency to be indifferent toward God to beat us down. On the contrary, the awareness of our great need should catalyze great boldness to "draw near to the throne of grace, that we may receive mercy and find grace to help in time of need" (Heb. 4:16). Instead, we can turn the preverbal log we once beat ourselves with into a battering ram against the gates of Hell! However, we will *only* have a courageous heart to overcome the enemy once our hearts become wonderfully overcome with the one thing in life we can't do without.

CHAPTER 12

COME DISTRACTED

"But one thing is necessary. Mary has chosen the good portion, which will not be taken away from her."

LUKE 10:42

With eyes fixated on the clock, I nervously paced around the room. Anxiety filled my heart. "What will I say?" I thought to myself. "Will I have anything at all to say?" Doubts dominated my mind. No matter how hard I studied or stressed, I was stuck. The hours seemed to evaporate. I was running out of time with less than 24 hours to develop a sermon from scratch. Worn out from worrying, I plopped down onto the couch. I said, "Father, I'm done trying; I'm just going to sit here with You. I don't know what else to do." As I literally held up my arms in surrender, I said, "Father, if for some reason You want to make a fool of me because I'll have nothing to say, then that's okay. I trust You. I'm willing to be a living sacrifice, whatever that looks like. Do what You want." Before I even finished speaking, I felt the sensation of warm, weightless snowflakes settling on me. I realize that such a thing doesn't exist, but I don't know how else to describe what I experienced. Peace and clarity gently descended upon my heart and mind. It was as if time stood still. I witnessed in the first person a manifestation of Philippians 4:6-7 (NKJV).

> "Be anxious for nothing, but in everything by prayer and supplication, with thanksgiving, let your requests be made known to God; and the peace of God, which surpasses all understanding, will guard your hearts and minds through Christ Jesus."

My heart and mind were under attack. Instead of surrendering to Jesus, at some point, I had succumbed to the deception that worrying somehow makes sense. I was unknowingly convinced with "logic" contrary to the Lord and thereby erected a demonic stronghold in my mind.

But something broke when I submitted myself to God. When I prayed, everything changed. The Prince of Peace came and brought the indescribable peace of His presence. God Himself stood like a sentry at the doorway of my spirit. (The expanded Greek definition of the word "guard" as used in Philippians 4:7 is: "to guard, protect by a military guard, either to prevent hostile invasion, or to keep the inhabitants of a besieged city from flight."[26])

Strongholds fall at Jesus's feet. They crumble there because only He has the power to break them. Try all you want on your own, but it's a lost cause without the Lord. On your own, your strongholds will stay, and nothing will change. But when we bow in the presence of the King, any unwelcome demonic tagalongs must also do so. It's time to defeat what defeats you. The spiritual forces of evil that had previously crippled your spirit can be crippled in the all-powerful presence of the Holy Spirit. God has given us everything necessary to transform our lives because "His divine power has granted to us *all things that pertain to life and godliness*" (1 Pet. 1:3a).

Even though other times during "pre-preaching warfare," I have had to flat out tell the devil to flee, in the particular battle I just described, all I did was simply reach out to God for help. He did the rest. He gave me rest. But that was just the beginning.

Suddenly, the Holy Spirit began rearranging and connecting Bible verses and life experiences in my mind, which were previously disorganized and seemingly disconnected. About 12 hours later, I miraculously had a coherent, Spirit-empowered sermon that would have usually taken me one to two weeks to assemble. It was only when I humbly yielded in the presence of Christ that the mind of Christ became manifest in me.

Initially unknown to me, the Father *didn't* want to humiliate me. He just wanted to help me, to work alongside me, because He knew I needed His help. Our Father loves to be involved in our lives; He's good like that. Jesus said, "For my yoke is easy, and my burden is light" (Matt. 11:30). No wonder John also said, "And his commandments are *not* burdensome" (1 John 5:3b). As my story illustrates, working with Jesus is always easier than trying to accomplish something independent of Him. Productivity aside, life is more fun with Jesus because the Father has anointed Him "with the oil of joy" more than anyone else (see Ps. 45:7 NASB).

Have you ever felt like something is missing in your life? What if the something you're missing is actually a Someone? Guess what? That Someone is missing you too. If you're a parent, you will likely relate to what I'm about to share.

Thrilled to spend time with them, I called out to my kids, "Hey everyone, let's hang out." "Not now, Dad," came the reply. "I need to finish my [smartphone app] game." My heart sank. With my head down, I said, "I miss you; I'd love to spend some time with you." There was no answer. My children were too distracted to hear their father's voice.

Thankfully, my kids came around, even though it took a few tries on my part. We have since ended that temporary season of allowing (pre-screened) app games without regret. Distractions crowd our twenty-first century lives. Statista reports, "Consumers around the world spend an average of 463 minutes or over 7.5 hours per day with media."[27] But no matter what vies for their attention, quality time with a loving parent will always impart more to a child than any distraction could ever do for them.

SIT AT HIS FEET, LOOK INTO HIS EYES

Despite everything we're all bombarded with daily, for young and old alike, what you and I need more than anything is found in one place. Just one. I cannot say that emphatically enough, but I didn't say it.

> "Now as they went on their way, Jesus entered a village. And a woman named Martha welcomed him into her house. And she had a sister called Mary, who sat at the Lord's feet and listened to his teaching. But Martha was distracted with much serving. And she went up to him and said, 'Lord, do you not care that my sister has left me to serve alone? Tell her then to help me.' But the Lord answered her, 'Martha, Martha, you are anxious and troubled about many things, but *one thing is necessary*. Mary has chosen the good portion, which will not be taken away from her'" (Luke 10:38–42).

Mary's response to Jesus was strikingly different from Martha's. Ironically, although Martha greeted Jesus at the door, she didn't pay much attention to Him once inside her house. Mary, however, made time for her Master. Sadly, Martha personifies the norm among many. Too often, many invite Jesus in as Savior and later ignore Him as their only Lord and greatest Love (see Matt. 10:37; Luke 14:26).

Martha was overly concerned with the things in her house. Mary was overtly content with the One who was her home.

Martha's "much serving" to look the part only served to camouflage a hidden war within. Mary, however, had peace within as she looked into Jesus's eyes.

Martha was overwhelmed at the thought that she might not be serving well enough. Mary was overjoyed and humbled to be perfectly served by the perfect One.

Martha was moving. Mary was moved.

Martha was dizzied with worry as she spun around on her feet, fearing that she might not gain Jesus's approval. Mary discovered rest at the feet of the One she knew accepted her. It was there that she experienced that "perfect love casts out fear" (see 1 John 4:18).

Martha hoped she was busy enough to be worthy enough of Jesus. Mary's identity and hope were anchored in the One who valued her more than even His own life (see Heb. 6:19-20).

Martha searched for something to satiate her heart's lack. Mary found ultimate satisfaction and joy by being loved by the One who loved her "with an everlasting love" (see Jer. 31:3). Moses expressed that reality in Psalm 90:14: "Satisfy us in the morning with your steadfast love, that we may rejoice and be glad all our days."

Martha lectured Jesus even though she didn't seem to hear His words. Mary listened to Jesus even though she probably didn't understand everything He said—her actions paralleled Simon Peter's words to Jesus: "Lord, to whom shall we go? You have the words of eternal life" (John 6:68b NIV).

Martha had much to say. Mary realized how much Jesus had to offer ("'To sit at the feet,' means to occupy the place of a learner (De 33:3; Lu 10:39; Ac 22:3).").[28] She knew that sitting at Jesus's feet is *not* optional; it's essential. Mary understood something: when we first let Jesus speak in our sitting, He will most powerfully move in our moving. Time with Jesus is not just nice-to-have but the ultimate must-have.

Martha strove to control things. Mary wholly submitted to Jesus's control over everything.

Martha tried to change things on her own. Mary came to the ultimate Game-Changer.

Martha was "troubled about many things" and consequently became captive to those things. Mary was captivated by "one thing" over anything and became the benefactor of everything.

Martha had a divided heart. Mary had a singularly devoted heart.

Martha had many loves. Mary had but one Love; as such, any previous loves had been, at best, reduced to likes.

Martha didn't see what Mary saw in "that Guy." Mary saw

Jesus looking at her as His "perfect one" (Song of Sol. 5:2b). Mary knew that "her sins, which are many, have been forgiven, for she loved much; but he who is forgiven little, loves little" (Luke 7:47).

Martha became so whipped up with worry that she even tried to drag Mary into her anxiety-motivated mess. But Martha's attempts to manipulate her sister didn't phase Mary. Martha's caustic words were no match for the words of life that flowed from Jesus's mouth. Mary just continued listening to her Master, receiving with ease from the One who had her affection.

Both sisters had something in common. They were both distracted—Martha with many things, but Mary with a single Someone.

I estimate that I've listened to more than 3,000 sermons. Over the years, I've attended many pastor and ministry leader conferences and Bible college courses, covering a wide range of worthwhile topics. But, as I recall, I can count on four or five fingers how many of those teachings, breakout sessions, and lectures were *solely dedicated* to the necessity of slowing down and spending time receiving from Jesus. Maybe your experience has differed from mine. But at least in my experience, how is it that the one thing *Jesus* said is essential is so woefully undertaught? If *Jesus* stated that "one thing is necessary," why is that one thing so often sidestepped?

If the devil fails to paralyze us with fear or beat us down with discouragement, he will simply try to distract us from what we need most. The enemy will gladly push us to talk about and even do *good* things to keep us from the *best* thing, from the one thing, from intimacy with Jesus.

No one is above the need to sit at the feet of God. Even Jesus frequently slipped away to pray and be alone with the Father—*especially* when life was busy, and His ministry was growing (see Mark 1:35; Luke 5:15-17).

When we care more about producing ministry than ministering to the Lord and letting Him minister to us, we bypass the only "Who" with whom we can produce the "what" (see John 15:5). Satan has enticed many with the allure of anything that *appears* godly but is nothing more than dead religion. Without the Spirit's leading and involvement, even our best "ministry" efforts will build nothing more than idols, be nothing more than "the work of human hands" (Ps. 115:4b), and amount to nothing more than "striving after wind" (see Eccles. 1:14). "*Unless the Lord builds the house*, those who build it labor in vain" (Ps. 127:1a).

WHAT IF YOU DON'T SEE WHAT MARY SAW?

What if, like Martha, you've worked hard for the Lord, yet your heart still feels cold? What if you're more like Martha than Mary? Is there any hope for you? The short answer is yes! Jesus was *not* trying to shame Martha with His words.

He was instead wooing her into the same rich blessing Mary was experiencing. Even if you are more like Martha than Mary, Jesus is still pulling you close.

But maybe you've prayed for change, and nothing seems to have shifted. Push through—don't give up. Even if you've hit a dead-end or feel like you're living in a spiritual wasteland, we serve the God who can miraculously make "a way in the wilderness and rivers in the desert" (Isa. 43:19b). Seek God with all your heart. While it includes praying, seeking is more than a rote, ritualistic task. In Matthew 7:7 (NIV), Jesus promised: "Ask and it *will* be given to you; seek and you *will* find; knock and the door *will* be opened to you." Do you believe that? If Jesus said it, it's true because "It is impossible for God to lie" (see Heb. 6:18 NIV). What if you even diligently read the Bible but, more often than not, the words on the page feel lifeless? Although it includes reading Scripture, seeking is different from mere learning. It's possible, even common, to read and yet not know. Are you pursuing Jesus the person or something else? Jesus said, "You study the Scriptures diligently because you think that in them you have eternal life. These are the very Scriptures that testify *about me,* yet you refuse to come *to me* to have life" (John 5:39-40 NIV). Are you parched in your soul? "Jesus stood and said in a loud voice, 'Let *anyone* who is thirsty come *to me* and drink'" (John 7:37b NIV). "Come, *everyone* who thirsts, come to the waters; and he who has no money, come, buy and eat" (Isa. 55:1a)! Jesus offers free living water that you won't find anywhere else—and you can drink as much as you desire!

Come Distracted

So what was Mary's secret? No secret. Not that it was a contest (it wasn't), but Mary just wanted *Jesus* more than her sister did. Mary was thirsty, and so she drank. The difference is that, while Martha did and desired many things, Mary was desperate for one thing: Jesus. As a result, when Jesus spoke, Mary's natural inclination was to cease anything competing with the voice of her beloved.

While Martha missed the moment, Mary stopped at a moment's notice to simply enjoy the moment and receive from Jesus. You'll connect with the Lord more deeply by responding *when* He has something for you *that you'll otherwise miss*. "Seek the Lord *while* He may be found; Call upon Him *while He is near*" (Isa. 55:6 NASB). Even if His timing *seems* off, the next time Jesus wants to speak to you, simply stop and listen, no matter how inconvenient. God's timing is always impeccable and always with good reason. Even if He knocks or nudges in the middle of the night, the middle of the day, or in the middle of something "important," the next time Jesus calls out, "Behold, I stand at the door and knock. If anyone hears my voice and opens the door,"—it's time to open the door, and when you do, as He said—"I will come in to him and eat with him, and he with me" (Rev. 3:20). Jesus spoke and is still speaking those living words to none other than His Church, His Bride.

No more would we ignore the person sitting across the table from us at dinner than should we disregard Jesus when He's in the room and has something to say. Instead, we should respond like David—"*When* You said, 'Seek My face,' My heart said to You, 'Your face, Lord, I will seek'" (Ps. 27:8 NKJV). The same God who sought David is also seeking you. The same Jesus who was available to Mary equally wanted to spend time with Martha.

Nevertheless, no matter how willing Jesus is to be with us, many still avoid Him as Martha did. Why is this? I believe it's ultimately because the original relationship wrecker, "the god of this age" (see 2 Cor. 4:4 NIV), has warped the culture of earth. Consequently, our society is often contrary to God's Kingdom culture—a culture built on love relationships with God and others (see Matt. 22:37-40). The unpredictability of a genuine relationship with Jesus makes many church-goers uncomfortable, which is a prime example of this culture clash. Many prefer to avoid anything unpredictable because they cannot control what they cannot predict. But the more we try to engineer our relationship with God to be predictable and within *our* control, the more we create a god (little "g") in our image. The longer anyone enables that sort of idolatry in their life, the less that person engages with the other Person in the relationship.

Without realizing it, we can fixate more on dissecting what abiding in Jesus is supposed to look like rather than remembering that it looks different for each person and varies daily.[29] As a result, many have shied away from what God intended to be a lifelong series of spontaneous interactions with a Friend.

Jesus eagerly waits for us to respond to His repeated invites for an authentic and thriving relationship. God is always ready to help us break through the rigid, lifeless concrete of self-made religion by the power of "Christ who is your life" (see Col. 2:23; 3:3-4).

Like any healthy relationship, walking with Jesus is inherently a two-way street. Jesus speaks; you respond. You speak; Jesus responds. In John 15, Jesus was abundantly clear that abiding in Him is *never* one-sided—as He said, "Abide in me," (our part) "and I in you" (Jesus's part). "If you abide in me, and my words abide in you, ask whatever you wish," (our part), "and it will be done for you" (Jesus's part). "Whoever abides in me" (our part) "and I in him" (Jesus's part), "he it is that bears much fruit, for apart from me you can do nothing" (sum of the parts) (see John 15:4a, 7, 5b).

God's design since Creation has been interactive, bi-lateral relationships with each individual He created. Even before the written Word of God existed, there was a walk with God "in the garden in the cool of the day" (see Gen. 3:8). God has had a common aim with all His words and actions since the fateful day His friends walked away from Him: to restore enduring, enjoyable, and fruitful relationships. No wonder, in His final prayer before the Cross, Jesus repeatedly asked that we "may be one" with Him, "*even as*" *He is one with the Father* (see John 17:11, 21, 22, 23). No matter how mind-boggling, that level of closeness with Jesus is not only possible, but it's also God's perfect design for you *now in this life* (not just someday in Heaven). I know this to be true because, in verse 23, Jesus prayed, "I in them and you in me, that they may become perfectly one, *so that the world may know that you sent me and loved them even as you loved me.*"

In the first person, God promises, "You will seek me and find me, *when you seek me with all your heart*" (Jer. 29:13). In other words, if you are half-hearted in your relationship with God (or if you don't yet have a relationship with Him), don't be surprised if you *don't* "find" Him. On the other hand, if you seek Jesus with *all* of your heart, you *will* find Him and discern when He is seeking you. And when that happens, something else will happen: your heart, mind, and life will start to change.

The more you "find" and fall in love with Jesus, the less you will fall for anything inferior to Him. The more you are satisfied by God's love for you, the less you will look for counterfeit satisfaction elsewhere. The more you "know the love of Christ that surpasses knowledge," the more you will "be filled with all the fullness of God" (see Eph. 3:19). The more full you are with God, the more His love will crowd out all other loves. If all I have ever known is stale mac 'n' cheese, how will my desires change once I experience something far better (the perfect ribeye steak, in my case)? Exactly, once I taste that better thing, there will be no going back. As "Jesus said to them, 'I am the bread of life; whoever comes to me shall not hunger, and whoever believes in me shall never thirst'" (John 6:35).

The more you "taste and see that the Lord is good" (Ps. 34:8a

NIV), the more hungry and thirsty you will be for Him. When we are smitten with Jesus, our natural response will be to seek Him like David did, who passionately declared in Psalm 27:4 (NKJV),

> "*One thing* I have desired of the Lord, That will I seek: That I may dwell in the house of the Lord All the days of my life, To behold the beauty of the Lord, And to inquire in His temple."

NOT EVERYONE WILL SEE WHAT MARY SAW

But the more we become enraptured with Jesus, the more we will be the target of ridicule from "Marthas" and "Elis." Religious people will often be nearby as we pour out our hearts and lives to God. You may recall the story from 1 Samuel 1:10-16 (NKJV) when barren Hannah begged the Lord for a son.

> "And she was in bitterness of soul, and prayed to the Lord and wept in anguish. Then she made a vow and said, 'O Lord of hosts, if You will indeed look on the affliction of Your maidservant and remember me, and not forget Your maidservant, but will give Your maidservant a male child, then I will give him to the Lord all the days of his life, and no razor shall come upon his head.' And it happened, as she continued praying before the Lord, that Eli watched her mouth. Now Hannah spoke in her heart; only her lips moved, but her voice was not heard. Therefore Eli thought she was drunk. So Eli said to her, 'How long will you be drunk? Put your wine away from

> you!' But Hannah answered and said, 'No, my lord, I am a woman of sorrowful spirit. I have drunk neither wine nor intoxicating drink, but have poured out my soul before the LORD. Do not consider your maidservant a wicked woman, for out of the abundance of my complaint and grief I have spoken until now.'"

Eli seems to have had at least one thing right: Hannah was drunk, but not with wine. She was instead intoxicated and impassioned in the presence of her God.

As you seek Jesus, you will be intercepted by those who care more about policing you rather than pursuing Jesus themselves. Expect it, but when that happens, know that you have an unseen enemy working behind the scenes which will stop at nothing to stop you from seeking the One *who* matters most. These are the words of the lovesick Shulamite woman and her experience in pursuit of her beloved (in Song of Solomon 5:4-9 NIV).

> "My beloved thrust his hand through the latch-opening; my heart began to pound for him. I arose to open for my beloved, and my hands dripped with myrrh, my fingers with flowing myrrh, on the handles of the bolt. I opened for my beloved, but my beloved had left; he was gone. My heart sank at his departure. I looked for him but did not find him. I called him but he did not answer. The watchmen found me as they made their rounds in the city. They beat me, they bruised me; they took away my cloak, those watchmen of the walls! Daughters of Jerusalem, I

charge you — if you find my beloved, what will you tell him? Tell him I am faint with love. How is your beloved better than others, most beautiful of women? How is your beloved better than others, that you so charge us?"

As you run to your first Love, your Beloved, your one thing, be encouraged by the resolve of Solomon's bride (the Shulamite woman). Remember how she unflinchingly followed her one Love, even when beaten by the watchmen.

As in Solomon's day, the disciplined watchmen of the New Testament Ephesian Church persevered but disturbingly left their first love in the process (see Rev. 2:3-4 NKJV). Throughout all these biblical accounts, there is something that Martha, Eli, religious watchmen, and even some of Jesus's disciples have in common. Isaiah wrote, "His watchmen are blind; they are all without knowledge; they are all silent dogs; they cannot bark, dreaming, lying down, loving to slumber" (Isa. 56:10). Instead of being awakened by the love of the Father to get up and seek Jesus, sadly, such individuals echo the same sentiment of Song of Solomon 5:9 (NIV)—"How is your beloved better than others, most beautiful of women? How is your beloved better than others, that you so charge us?" Christian or not, I am convinced that anyone who doesn't understand why you are so in love with Jesus has not yet drunk deeply, intimately, of that same love themselves.

Like the Shulamite woman, Mary was also in love with her Lord. The book of Matthew (26:6-16) recounts the story like this,

> "Now when Jesus was at Bethany in the house of Simon the leper, a woman came up to him with an alabaster flask of very expensive ointment, and she poured it on his head as he reclined at table. And when the disciples saw it, they were indignant, saying, 'Why this waste? For this could have been sold for a large sum and given to the poor.' But Jesus, aware of this, said to them, 'Why do you trouble the woman? For she has done a beautiful thing to me. For you always have the poor with you, but you will not always have me. In pouring this ointment on my body, she has done it to prepare me for burial. Truly, I say to you, wherever this gospel is proclaimed in the whole world, what she has done will also be told in memory of her.' Then one of the twelve, whose name was Judas Iscariot, went to the chief priests and said, 'What will you give me if I deliver him over to you?' And they paid him thirty pieces of silver. And from that moment he sought an opportunity to betray him."

Judas had had enough. He was indignant that Mary wasted something so valuable on a pauper from Nazareth. Interestingly, the expression of such lavish love toward Jesus was the straw that broke the camel's back for Judas.

Those who *passionately* love Jesus will either estrange or endear you to God—because if Jesus doesn't overjoy you, He will inevitably offend you. Lackluster affection for Jesus is a telltale symptom of spiritual adultery. Solomon wisely argued, "Drink water from your own cistern, flowing water from your own well. Should your springs be scattered abroad, streams of water in the streets" (Prov. 5:15-16)? For who or what are you pouring out your resources, your time, your love? If it's not Jesus, you can start moving in the right direction by just getting alone with Him.

WHY IS BEING WITH JESUS THE ULTIMATE LIFE-CHANGER?

How can simply spending time with Jesus change your life? Because you will become like whoever you hang out with—simple as that. If "bad company corrupts good character" (1 Cor. 15:33b NIV), what could keeping the *best* company do for you?!

Have you ever known someone to be so discouraged that they became despondent? Instead of pressing on, they gave up. They were asleep at the wheel when needed most. I'm familiar with a group of individuals who did just that and even worse. The particular people I'm thinking of eventually became so fearful of the world around them that they decided to stay holed up in their homes. I'm referring to Jesus's disciples, who were "sleeping for sorrow" and later became shut-ins "for fear of the Jews" when they should have been boldly praying and out proclaiming Jesus (see Luke 22:45; John 20:19). Thankfully, their stories didn't end there. Fast-forward to the birth of the Church as recorded in the early chapters of Acts.

Peter and John had been arrested and imprisoned for publicly healing a man and "proclaiming in Jesus the resurrection from the dead," resulting in more than 5,000 souls saved (see Acts 3:1-10; 4:2-4). Wow, what a couple of months can bring!

The same individuals previously grounded by discouragement and gripped with fear later displayed staggering courage and boldness, even when facing persecution and threats (see Acts 4:5-22).

How did Peter and John experience such a drastic life transformation? Their haters knew the answer:

> "Now when they saw the boldness of Peter and John, and perceived that they were uneducated, common men, they were astonished. *And they recognized that they had been with Jesus*" (Acts 4:13).

People sometimes say, "But it can't be that simple." Peter and John would beg to differ. Even the Pharisees would disagree. Jesus told Martha otherwise: while there are *many important things*, there's only *one necessary thing*. I, for one, am thankful it's that simple.

Someone once said, "Show me your friends, and I'll show you your future." Jesus invites you into a friendship beyond anything you've ever known: "No longer do I call you servants, for a servant does not know what his master is doing; but I have called you friends" (John 15:15a NKJV). Is your relationship with Jesus limited to you as His servant (which we are)? Or have you reciprocated His friendship? Peter and John did, and it forever changed the trajectory of their lives.

No one else, nothing else, can transform your life like Jesus. He is the Creator and the only source of all power and true love (see John 1:1-3, 14; Phil. 2:9-10; Col. 1:17; 1 John 4:7, 10). What could more time around such powerful love do for your heart, your mind, your life? How courageously will you resist the devil next time he messes with you and those around you?

Everything flows downstream from love, from your intimate love connection with Jesus (see John 15:4-5; 17:3). When our love relationship with Jesus is out of whack, everything else will be—our thoughts, words, actions. Nothing will activate and empower us more than an abiding awareness of the Father's love and grace for us.

The reality is that soldiers who forget that they are first beloved daughters and sons will never fight well, if at all. When Jesus came, lived, died, resurrected, and ascended for you, He did so not just as Almighty but to also reveal Abba (Father). "See what kind of love the Father has given to us, that *we should be called children of God; and so we are*" (1 John 3:1a). Because God has always wanted you, you can now have the Father you've always wanted.

Nothing in all creation can awaken sleeping minds, thaw cold hearts, and transform tattered lives like the undying, all-powerful, indescribable love of God. When you are captivated by the Father's incomparable love for you, you become compelled to do things you wouldn't otherwise do. When you are in love with someone, really in love, nothing else matters in comparison. You will do anything, endure anything, even give anything for them. When we are all-in on Jesus, His passion and love for others will spill out of us.

Friendship with Jesus is what yields fruitfulness for Jesus. That's what Jesus spoke of when He said, "You are my friends if you do what I command." What command? "My command is this: Love each other as I have loved you" (John 15:14, 12 NIV). Friendship with God is the greenhouse in which His seeds of love germinate and later produce fruit in the soil of life. We cannot walk out what Jesus commands unless we first walk with Him as our friend. Only once you experience God's love *for you personally* can you lead others to that same God of love. Read what Paul penned in 2 Corinthians 5:14-15 (NIV).

> "For *Christ's love compels us*, because we are convinced that one died for all, and therefore all died. And he died for all, that those who live should no longer live for themselves but for him who died for them and was raised again."

When you genuinely love God—knowing how much He loves you—surrendering to Him, submitting to Him, will come naturally. On the other hand, if you're *not* in love with Jesus, "submit" will seem like a dirty six-letter word. Everyone is ultimately submissive to someone or something: Satan and sin, or the Savior. The first two are cruel masters; there is only one kind and good Master: Jesus.

Only when you and I submit to God will we gain the strength

to effectively counter the enemy. Resisting the devil is wholly rooted in your reliance on God. Listen to what the Holy Spirit said through one of Jesus's brothers: "But he gives more grace. Therefore it says, 'God opposes the proud but gives grace to the humble.' Submit yourselves therefore to God. Resist the devil, and he will flee from you" (James 4:6-7). Notice what precedes submitting to Jesus or even resisting the devil: God's grace, His love. God's great mercy is what motivates us to continually present our lives as living sacrifices for God's service. Paul pleaded, "I appeal to you therefore, brothers, *by the mercies of God*, to present your bodies as a living sacrifice, holy and acceptable to God, which is your spiritual worship" (Rom. 12:1). He also wrote this to Titus (2:11-14 NKJV) –

> "For *the grace of God* that brings salvation has appeared to all men, teaching us that, denying ungodliness and worldly lusts, we should *live soberly, righteously, and godly in the present age*, looking for the blessed hope and glorious appearing of our great God and Savior Jesus Christ, *who gave Himself for us*, that He might redeem us from every lawless deed and purify for Himself His own special people, *zealous for good works.*"

The same grace of God that first drew us to God *should* also propel us to "be sober-minded" in order to "resist" the devil (see 1 Pet. 5:8-9), to live for our living King, and further the Father's Kingdom.

As you enjoy God's love for you and submit to Him, the

natural progression should be a growing compulsion to war for yourself and those you might otherwise overlook. Never stop short of actively resisting the devil whenever you perceive him at work. Because if you avoid countering the enemy, you'll be confused why you can't experience lasting change in your life, and the lives of others. Failing to engage the right enemy the right way (e.g., wielding God's Word, praying in the Spirit, casting out demons) should never keep you from winning spiritual battles. May what was often true of ancient Israel *not* be our reality: "They have blown the trumpet and made everything ready, *but none goes to battle*" (Ezek. 7:14a).

It's time to wage war against our adversary… and win.

It's time to stop sidestepping spiritual realities that Jesus addressed head-on.

It's time for the Lord—our "defense" and almighty "warrior" (see Exod. 15:2-3)—to become our battle plan.

It's time to ditch anything that distracts from the "one thing" as we experience the love of Jesus more than ever before.

It's time for something better, for Someone better.

It's time to see Jesus's face so we can discern how to follow His feet.

It's time for a change.

NOTES

1. "G3823—Palē—Strong's Greek Lexicon (Esv)". 2020. *Blue Letter Bible*. https://www.blueletterbible.org/lexicon/g3823/esv/mgnt/0-1/.
2. "Ben-Hadad—Wikipedia". 2020. *En.Wikipedia.Org*. https://en.wikipedia.org/wiki/Ben-hadad.
3. The number of horror movies produced each year can be viewed and compared by replacing "{year}" with the year number (e.g., 2019) in the following URL: https://www.the-numbers.com/market/{year}/genres
4. "Genres Movie Breakdown For 2021". 2021. *The Numbers*. https://www.the-numbers.com/market/2021/genres.
5. "Genres Movie Breakdown For 2020". 2020. *The Numbers*. https://www.the-numbers.com/market/2020/genres.
6. Vannatta, Allyson. 2020. "Study: Americans Turn To TV And Movies Instead Of Their Faith To Deal With Pandemic". *Movieguide*. https://www.movieguide.org/news-articles/study-americans-turn-to-tv-and-movies-instead-of-their-faith-to-deal-with-pandemic.html.
7. Fairchild, Mary. 2020. "Essential Stats And Facts About Christianity Today". *Learn Religions*. https://www.learnreligions.com/christianity-statistics-700533.
8. Ahmad, Farida B., and Robert N. Anderson. 2021. "The Leading Causes Of Death In The US For 2020". *JAMA Network*. https://jamanetwork.com/journals/jama/fullarticle/2778234.
9. Ducharme, Jamie. 2019. "More Millennials Are Dying 'Deaths Of Despair,' As Overdose And Suicide Rates Climb". *Time*. https://time.com/5606411/millennials-deaths-of-despair/.
10. "God" within brackets has been added by the author in place of "he".
11. "Jesus" within brackets has been added by the author.

12. "His" within brackets has been added by the author in place of "Your".
13. "the Lord" within brackets has been added by the author.
14. Spafford, Horatio Gates. 1873. "When Peace, Like A River". *Hymnary.Org*. https://hymnary.org/text/when_peace_like_a_river_attendeth_my_way.
15. Sammis, John Henry. 1887. "Hymn: Trust And Obey". *Hymnal.Net*. https://www.hymnal.net/en/hymn/h/582.
16. Read the full story in 2 Chron. 20:1-30.
17. This was calculated from the number of words in the Lord's Prayer—from Matthew 9b-13—based on the NKJV translation of the Bible.
18. See 1 Timothy 5:1 as an example of encouragement used for corrective purposes.
19. Utley, Bob. 2012. "Introduction To Philippians | Bible.Org". *Bible.Org*. https://bible.org/seriespage/introduction-philippians.
20. In most of his letters to the churches (Romans, 1 Corinthians, 2 Corinthians, Ephesians, Philippians, and Colossians), Paul greeted Christian believers as "saints." In his other three church epistles (Galatians, 1 Thessalonians, and 2 Thessalonians), Paul addressed his fellow believers as "the churches" or just "the church."
21. "G40—Hagios—Strong's Greek Lexicon (Esv)". 2020. *Blue Letter Bible*. https://www.blueletterbible.org/lexicon/g40/esv/mgnt/0-1/.
22. "G1097—ginōskō—Strong's Greek Lexicon (Esv)". 2022. *Blue Letter Bible*. https://www.blueletterbible.org/lexicon/g1097/esv/mgnt/0-1/.
23. "H6960—Qāvâ—Strong's Hebrew Lexicon (Esv)". 2021. *Blue Letter Bible*. https://www.blueletterbible.org/lexicon/h6960/esv/wlc/0-1/.
24. "H79—'Ābaq—Strong's Hebrew Lexicon (Esv)". 2021. *Blue Letter Bible*. https://www.blueletterbible.org/lexicon/h79/esv/wlc/0-1/.
25. "who" within brackets has been added by the author.
26. "G5432—Phroureō—Strong's Greek Lexicon (Nkjv)". 2022. *Blue Letter Bible*. https://www.blueletterbible.org/lexicon/g5432/nkjv/tr/0-1/.
27. "Topic: Media Use In The U.S.". 2021. *Statista*. https://www.statista.com/topics/1536/media-use/#dossierKeyfigures.
28. Luering, H. "Foot—International Standard Bible Encyclopaedia." 2003. *Blue Letter Bible*. https://www.blueletterbible.org/search/dictionary/viewtopic.cfm?topic=IT0003503.
29. As several cases in point, see the varied human examples of faith in Hebrews 11.

NOTE TO READER

NOW WHAT?

Thank you for purchasing *Sidestepped: What the Enemy Doesn't Want You to Know That Can Change Your Life.*

If you've been encouraged by this book or audiobook, so will others. Please take a few moments to rate and review it at your favorite website. Invite your friends, family, and connections to get the book or audiobook. The short time you invest today to spread the word could impact many lives for years to come. Now is the time to fight *together*, to arise and say "no!" to the devil as we offer our "yes!" to the victorious King of Kings.

Yours in the Fight,
Matt

AVAILABLE SOON...

The next book in the *Sidestepped* series.

Scan the following QR code...

...to visit seekpress.us

Sign up for specials, get notified of upcoming book releases, and invite Matt to speak to your church or at your event.

ABOUT THE AUTHOR

MATT DALBEY is an author, speaker, businessman, husband, and father. From pastoring and teaching to leading home groups, discipleship, and community outreach, Matt has periodically served in various ministry capacities since 1999. Based on biblical reality, his writing embodies a unique relatability, courage, and timeliness for our generation. Matt and his wife have three children and live in the Pacific Northwest.

SEEKPRESS.US

SEEK PRESS™

Made in the USA
Monee, IL
15 March 2023